# American Inside Out Evolution

Student's Book | Pre-Intermediate | A

SUE KAY
VAUGHAN JONES
PHILIP KERR

macmillan education

Macmillan Education
Companies and representatives throughout the world
American Inside Out Evolution. Student's Book Pre-Intermediate A


Adapted by Peter Maggs and Catherine Smith / The Content Station team: Simon Campbell, George Wells, and Catherine Gray
Macmillan is a registered trademark.
First edition published 2017

ISBN: 978-607-473-649-6

Based on New American Inside Out Student's Book Pre-Intermediate A
D.R. © Macmillan Publishers, S.A. de C.V. 2009
Published under license from Macmillan Publishers Ltd.



Editorial Manager: Patricia Muradas
Editorial Operations Coordinator: Veronica Teodorov Ferreira
Editor: Cintia Zaitune
Concept design: Martha Tadaieski
Page make-up: The Content Station
Illustrations: Karen Ahlschläger pp15, 23, 25, 27, 29, 31, 33, 46, 64, 66, 71, 73, 75; Gustavo Gialuca pp14, 22, 30, 42, 50, 58; Roberto Weigand pp15, 31, 33.
Graphic Production: Kelly Gobbo
Photographic research: The Content Station
Cover concept and design: Jean Aranha
Cover photo: Svetlana195| Dreamstime

The authors and publishers would like to thank the following for permission to reproduce their photographs:

**Dreamstime** / Monkey Business Images p8, Dreamstime / Sergey Khakimullin p9(l), Dreamstime / Oksun70 p9(rt), Dreamstime / Ljupco p9(rc), Dreamstime / Nikolay Klimenko p9(rb), Dreamstime / Ruslan Huzau p10(1), Dreamstime / Ocusfocus p10(2), Dreamstime / Meinzahn p10(3), Dreamstime / Wavebreakmedia Ltd p10(4), Dreamstime / Hongqi Zhang (aka Michael Zhang) p10(5), Dreamstime / Stephen Coburn p10(6), Dreamstime / Wavebreakmedia Ltd p10(7), Dreamstime / Yurolaitsalbert p10(8), Dreamstime / Nenitorx p10(9), Dreamstime / Gunold p11(5), Dreamstime / Willis Shackleford p11(4), Dreamstime / Natalia Lebedinskaia p11(3), Dreamstime / Otrokovice p11(2), Dreamstime / Khvainatskaya Tatsiana p11(1), Dreamstime / Msphotographic p12, Dreamstime / ProductionPerig p13, Dreamstime / Olga Mandzyuk p16 (Venice), Dreamstime / Sergey Kelin p16 (La Bastide), Dreamstime / Mauricio Jordan De Souza Coelho p16 (Rio), Dreamstime / Kadettmann p17 (Paulo), Dreamstime / Luanateutzi p17 (Armeile), Dreamstime / Andrey Popov p17 (Luigi), Dreamstime / Ifeelstock p17(b), Dreamstime / Vitaliy Tsvetkov p18(t), Dreamstime / Jcfotografo p18(bl), Dreamstime / VanderWolfImages p18(br), Dreamstime / Yurolaitsalbert p19 (pamelafox), Dreamstime / Mocker p19 (lisa22), Dreamstime / Andreblais p19 (rachel101), Dreamstime / Simon Greig p19 (tommydoe), Dreamstime / Dmitriy Shironosov p20, Dreamstime / Koseckil1 p21(t), Dreamstime / Candybox Images p22(b), Dreamstime / Yulia Ryabokon p23(1), Dreamstime / Yulia Ryabokon p23(2), Dreamstime / Lar01joka p23(3), Dreamstime / Jemastock p23(4), Dreamstime / Yehor Vlasenko p23(5), Dreamstime / Anastasiia Malysheva p23(6), Dreamstime / Ylivdesign p23(7), Dreamstime / Yael Weiss p23(8), Dreamstime / Pretoperola p24(c), Dreamstime / Solarisys13 p24(r), Dreamstime / Dechev p26 (Get Personal), Dreamstime / Elnur p26 (cooking show), Dreamstime / Stephanie Swartz p27(c), Dreamstime / 55hasan p27(b), Dreamstime / Anikasalsera p28(a), Dreamstime / Monkey Business Images p28(b), Dreamstime / Dzmitri Mikhaltsov p28(c), Dreamstime / Pavel Losevsky p28(d), Dreamstime / Mada Jimmy p28(e), Dreamstime / Andrey Armyagov p28(f), Dreamstime / Lyudmila Menshov p28 (house), Dreamstime / Monkey Business Images p29(b), Dreamstime / Iryna Kalchenko p30(a), Dreamstime / Wavebreakmedia Ltd p30(b), Dreamstime / Hootie2710 p30(c), Dreamstime / Scaliger p32, Dreamstime / Thirumurugan Ponnusamy p33(b), Dreamstime / Alexey Sinelnikov p34(tl), Dreamstime / Sebastian Czapnik p34(tr), Dreamstime / Subbotina p34(b), Dreamstime / Anton Maltsev p35(t), Dreamstime / Mirko Vitali p35(cl), Dreamstime / Rido p35(cr), Dreamstime / Ruslan Huzau p35(bl), Dreamstime / Anna Om p35(br), Dreamstime / Pisit Koolplukpol p36 (flowers), Dreamstime / Bert Folsom p36 (coffee), Dreamstime / Aimy27feb p36 (rose), Dreamstime / Vadymvdrobot p36 (Rosa), Dreamstime / Tmcphotos p36 (Jill), Dreamstime / Aetherial p36 (Dave), Dreamstime / Phovoir p36 (Carrie), Dreamstime / Kurhan p36 (Phil), Dreamstime / Mimagephotography p36 (Fred), Dreamstime / Stepanov p36 (Gina), Dreamstime / Mycolors p37(l), Dreamstime / Vladislav Kochelaevskiy p37(r), Dreamstime / Axel Bueckert p38(tl), Dreamstime / Ew Chee Guan p38(tr), Dreamstime / Sandra Cunningham p38(b), Dreamstime / Mystock88photo p39(bl), Dreamstime / Monkey Business Images p39(br), Dreamstime / Fashionstock .com p40(tl), Dreamstime / Fashionstock .com p40(tr), Dreamstime / Vitali Enhelbrekht p40(a), Dreamstime / Jacques Jacobsz p40(b), Dreamstime / Melonstone p40(c), Dreamstime / Costasz p40(d), Dreamstime / Fashionstock .com p41(t), Dreamstime / Elnur p43(1), Dreamstime / Vadim Shumiakov p43(2), Dreamstime / Tatyanaego p43(3), Dreamstime / Newlight p43(4), Dreamstime / Tatyanaego p43(5), Dreamstime / Rohit Seth p43(6), Dreamstime / Kai Siong Wong p43(7), Dreamstime / Flynt p43(8), Dreamstime / Ires007 p43(9), Dreamstime / Yap Kee Chan p43(10), Dreamstime / Gekaskr p43(11), Dreamstime / Andrey Simonenko p43(12), Dreamstime / Zstockphotos p44, Dreamstime / Nyul p45(t), Dreamstime / Brainsil p45(b), Dreamstime / Jenta Wong p47(rt), Dreamstime / Platongkoh p47(rb), Dreamstime / Travnikovstudio p48(l), Dreamstime / Threeart p48(r), Dreamstime / Vadymvdrobot p49, Dreamstime / Undrey p50(1), Dreamstime / Lunamarina p50(2), Dreamstime / Odua p50(3), Dreamstime / Denys Kurbatov p50(4), Dreamstime / Zts p50(5), Dreamstime / Gstockstudio1 p50(6), Dreamstime / Viovita p51 (trunks), Dreamstime / Volodymyr Shevchuk p51 (helmet), Dreamstime / Kati Finell p51 (clubs), Dreamstime / Veniamin Kraskov p51 (cleats), Dreamstime / Marusea Turcu p51 (racket), Dreamstime / Supertrooper p51 (shoes), Dreamstime / Juan Moyano p51 (net), Dreamstime / Fibobjects p51 (goggles), Dreamstime / Gemphotography p52(a), Dreamstime / Jkha p52(b), Dreamstime / Tyler Olson p52(c), Dreamstime / Elena Nichizhenova p52(d), Dreamstime / Terng99 p53, Dreamstime / Tyler Olson p54(t), Dreamstime / Lightkeeper p54(c), Dreamstime / Alexbutko p54 (Dan), Dreamstime / Andy Nowack p54 (Saskia), Dreamstime / Sireonio p54 (Sam), Dreamstime / Monkey Business Images p54 (Pete), Dreamstime / Wavebreakmedia Ltd p54 (Tim), Dreamstime / Wavebreak Media Ltd p55, Dreamstime / Anna Lurye p56(t), Dreamstime / Hongqi Zhang (aka Michael Zhang) p56(b), Dreamstime / Ruslan Huzau p57(t), Dreamstime / Fsstock p57(b), Dreamstime / .shock p58(b), Dreamstime / Iakov Filimonov p59(1), Dreamstime / Mainephotonut p59(2), Dreamstime / Victorrustle p59(3), Dreamstime / Denys Kovtun p59(4), Dreamstime / Phatthanit Roengsamran p59(5), Dreamstime / Iurii Stepanov p59(6), Dreamstime / Believeinme p59(7), Dreamstime / Unteroffizier p59(8), Dreamstime / Theripper p59(9), Dreamstime / Aleksey Boldin p59(10), Dreamstime / Ka2shka p59(11), Dreamstime / Mirage3 p59(12), Dreamstime / Wisconsinart p59(13), Dreamstime / Zimmytws p59(14), Dreamstime / Mohamed Osama p59(15), Dreamstime / Michael Drager p59(16), Dreamstime / Martinmark p60, Dreamstime / Migutas p61 (chocolates), Dreamstime / James Rooney p61 (beans), Dreamstime / Sirup p61 (keys), Dreamstime / Pichayasri p61 (perfume), Dreamstime / Iuliia Belenkova p61 (paint), Dreamstime / Snellie78 p61 (tissues), Dreamstime / Pichayasri p61 (flowers), Dreamstime / Stas11 p61 (water), Dreamstime / Mimagephotography p62(tl), Dreamstime / Poznyakov p62(tr), Dreamstime / Steven Cukrov p62(bl), Dreamstime / Stockyimages p62(br), Dreamstime / Pojoslaw p63(tr), Dreamstime / Vadymvdrobot p63(tl), Dreamstime / 2mmedia2011 p63(b), Dreamstime / Wieslaw Jarek p131, Dreamstime / Ahmad Zaihan Amran p138, Dreamstime / Hongqi Zhang (aka Michael Zhang) p139, Dreamstime / Rainer Lesniewski p141 (map), Dreamstime / Sergey Toropov p141 (flag); **Getty Images** / Fox Photos / Stringer p24(l), Getty / FOX / Contributor p26 (Bones), Getty / CBS Photo Archive / Contributor p26 (Big Bang Theory), Getty / Bloomberg / Contributor p39(tr), Getty / Axelle/Bauer-Griffin / Contributor p41(b), Getty / Ian Walton / Staff p46(a), Getty / Stuart Franklin / Staff p46(b), Getty / Clive Brunskill / Staff p46(c), Getty / VCG / Contributor p46(d), Getty / Giuseppe Bellini / Stringer p46(e), Getty / Sandro Pereyra / Stringer p46(f), Getty / Power Sport Images / Contributor p47(l)

CANIEM No. 2275

Macmillan Publishers S.A. de C.V.
Insurgentes Sur 1886
Col. Florida, CP 01030
Álvaro Obregón
Ciudad de México
Tel: +52 (55) 5482 2200
elt@grupomacmillan.com

www.grupomacmillan.com www.macmillan.com.mx www.macmillanenglish.com



Printed in Brazil

This book was printed in December, 2017 by: Eskenazi Indústria Gráfica Ltda, Avenida Miguel Frias Vasconcelos, 1023 - Jaguaré - São Paulo - SP.

# Contents

# Walkthrough

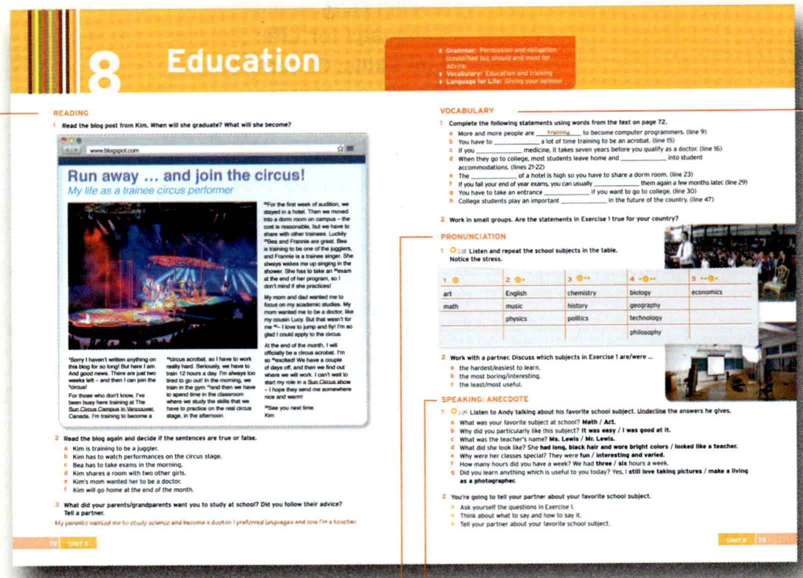

## READING

Contemporary reading texts have been adapted and graded to suit each level. They have been selected not only for their language content but also for their interest and appropriacy. The texts are supported by recordings.

## VOCABULARY

- Vocabulary is presented in a meaningful context and is related to the topics in the unit.
- Clear pictures to help acquisition.
- There are practice activities to expand your knowledge of particular lexical sets and that will give you opportunities to use the new vocabulary in social exchanges.
- You will also listen to the words and repeat them before manipulating them in real social contexts.

## PRONUNCIATION

Pronunciation work on particular areas of sound, stress, and intonation is integrated into every unit.

## SPEAKING

You will have plenty of opportunities to speak throughout the unit using language learned.

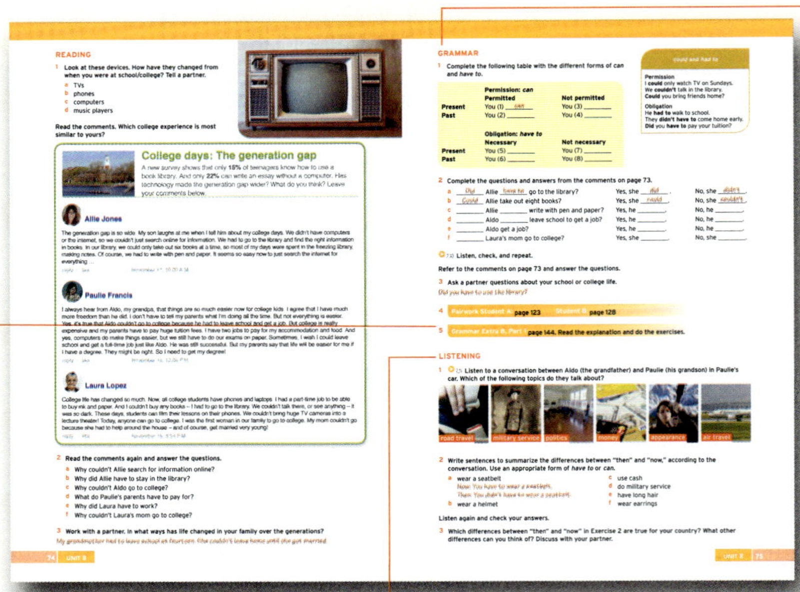

The Grammar Extra pages at the back of the Student's Book extend explanations and provide further practice.

## GRAMMAR

- Here you will explore new grammatical structures that have been contextualized in the reading / listening sections. You will focus on the way language works.
- A brief summary of the grammar point is provided in the margin.
- Language is explored in realistic and meaningful practice exercises.
- You will use target language in controlled and personalized practice.

## LISTENING

The listening activities include texts specially written for language learning – dialogues, conversations, and monologues. They were carefully designed to develop real-life listening skills.

## LANGUAGE FOR LIFE

The Language for Life section gives you a portable toolkit of functional language. Here, you notice how language is more than just form. You will see language in fun, engaging social situations.

## VOCABULARY EXTRA

The Vocabulary Extra pages at the end of every unit recycle the key vocabulary items taught in the unit. This provides an activated wordlist and a useful bank of vocabulary.

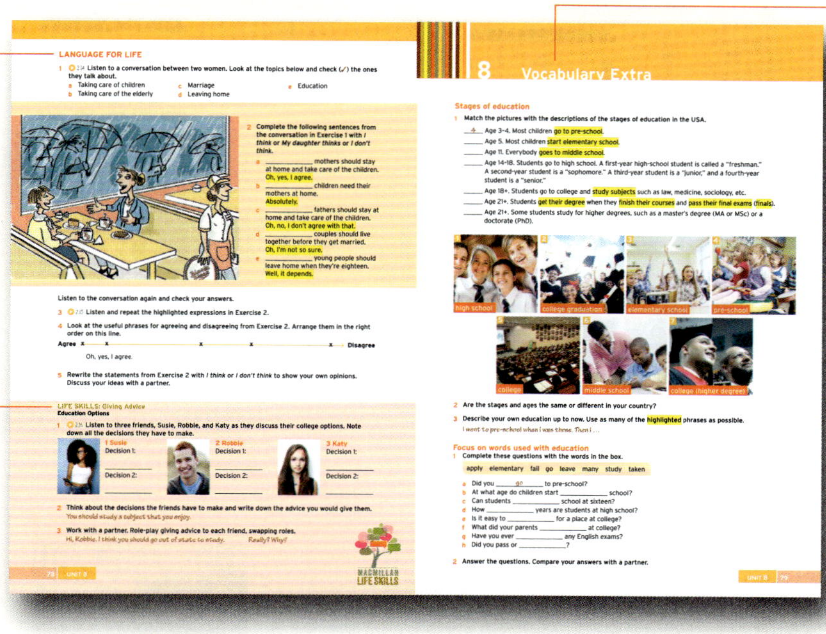

## LIFE SKILLS

Developing life skills alongside language skills is an essential requirement to meet the demands of the contemporary world.
*American Inside Out Evolution* has a Life Skills section in every unit. Life Skills present activities in order for you to reflect on and discuss the skills you need for social and work situations in today's world.

## REVIEW

There are Review units in the Student's Book. They review the new structures and vocabulary taught in the previous teaching units.

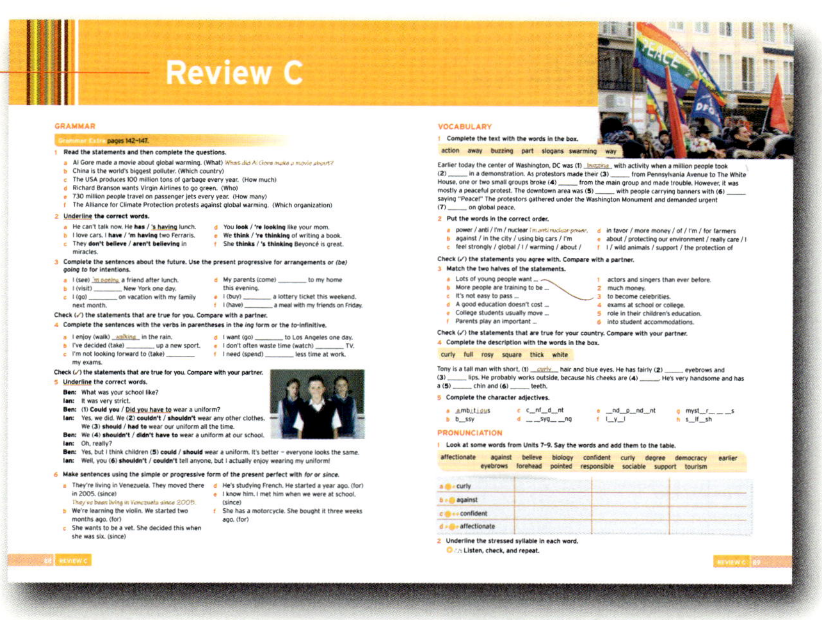

There is one Pairwork activity for every unit, which offers further speaking practice.

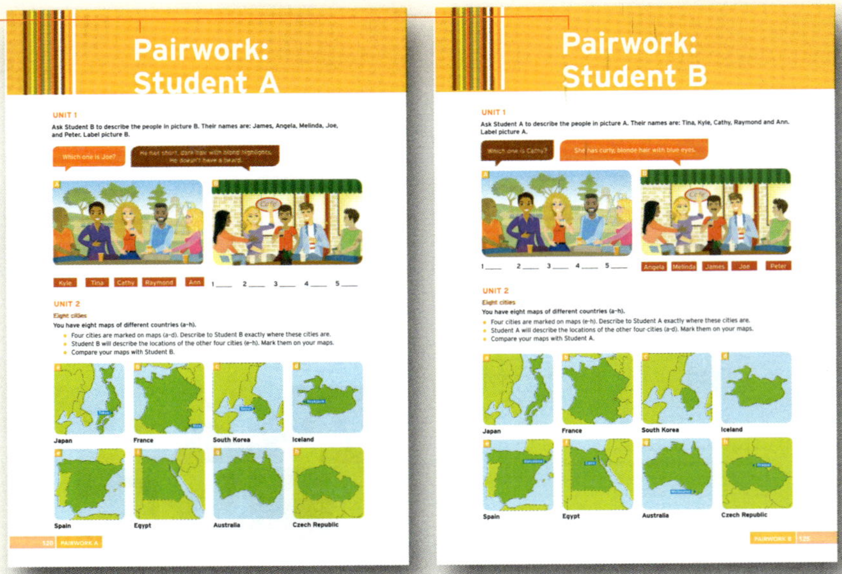

Pairwork: Student A

Pairwork: Student B

**GRAMMAR EXTRA**

The Grammar Extra pages at the back of the Student's Book provide a summary of the new grammatical structures, as well as extra practice.

Grammar Extra

The Workbook provides a review of all the main points in the Student's Book, plus extra listening practice, pronunciation work, and a writing program.

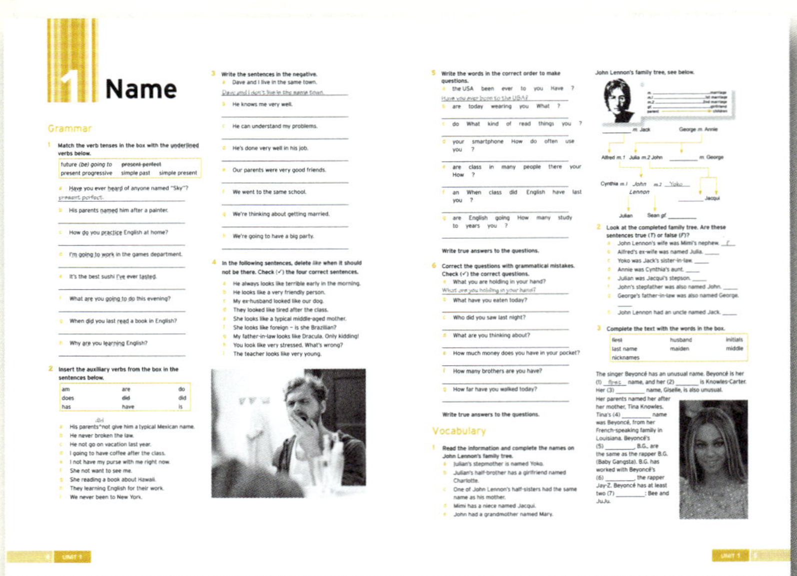

1 Name

# Student's Components

Student's Book with access code to Digital Student's Book

Workbook with access code to Digital Workbook

# 1 Name

## LISTENING

1 1.02 **Listen to two people talking about their names. Underline the four names you hear for each person.**

| **The man** | | | | | **The woman** | | | | |
|---|---|---|---|---|---|---|---|---|---|
| Benjamin | Ben | Benji | Tree | Big Ben | Maria | Anna-Maria | Mumu | Mimi | Baby |

2 **Complete these sentences with the words in the box.**

a His *parents* call him Benjamin.
b His _____ call him Tree.
c His _____ call him Big Ben.
d Her _____ call her Anna-Maria.
e Her _____ call her Maria.
f Her _____ calls her Baby.

brother English friends Mexican friends old friends parents sisters

## VOCABULARY

1 1.03 **Listen and repeat the words in the box.**

aunt boyfriend brother brother-in-law cousin daughter father girlfriend grandfather grandmother half-brother half-sister mother nephew niece sister sister-in-law son stepfather stepmother uncle

2 **Complete the table with words from Exercise 1. Where possible, add the first name of a person from your family as an example.**
**Tell your partner about some of the people in your family.**

| ♂ **Male** | ♀ **Female** |
|---|---|
| *boyfriend = No* | *aunt = Pilar* |
| *brother = Paco* | ________ |
| ________ | ________ |
| ________ | ________ |

I don't have a boyfriend. My brother's name is Diego. He's a student. He lives in Quito ...

3 **Work with a partner. Look at your names in Exercise 2 and discuss these questions.**

a Which names are typical in your country?
b Which name is the most unusual?
c Which name do you like best?

- **Grammar:** Tense review. *looks/looks like.* Question forms.
- **Vocabulary:** Family. Description. Names.
- **Language for Life:** Showing interest

## READING

1 **How did your parents choose your name? Was it for one of the reasons below or for a different reason? Tell a partner.**

a Your parents named you after a relative.
b They named you after a place.
c They chose an unusual name.
d They named you after a famous person.
e Your name is religious.
f It has a special meaning.
g Your parents simply liked the name.

2 **Read the post. Which of the reasons (a-g) is not mentioned?**

**Jennifer Ellis**
43 minutes ago

Hi all, just an update on our new baby! She's doing really well. We brought her home from the hospital last week and for the first time we got some sleep last night. Yay!

So, we haven't chosen a name. Still! And we're having arguments about it. Help! This is the problem. My parents named me after my grandmother, Jenny. Jennifer is our family name. My brother and his wife have three boys and they aren't going to have any more children. So, we need to keep this name in our family. And I think Jennifer is a good choice, right? Well, not so quick — Noah doesn't agree! He thinks it's going to be confusing to have two Jennifers in the house.

My partner is Noah because his parents are religious, and picked a name from the bible. And they think our baby should also have a biblical name – maybe Ruth or Eve. These are nice names, but I'm not sure they are right. I also want to choose something that is special to Noah and me, and not just choose names that are from a book.

We could name her after a place we like – Noah likes Japan, but I'm not sure Tokyo Ellis is right. And I like China, but I don't think it's a good idea to use any place names from there!

So, what should we do? Name her after my relative, pick a religious name, or is there another option …?

Like Comment Share

**Leo Richardson** Glad the baby is doing well! My parents named me after Leonardo DiCaprio – so maybe you can name the new baby after a famous person? I know you like Taylor Swift …!

Like · Reply · 1 · 22 minutes ago

**Caia Smith** Jen — please don't do what my parents did! They wanted an unusual name, so they chose a Roman goddess. Thanks, guys … It's no fun having a name like this. No one can say or spell it!

Like · Reply · 1 · 11 minutes ago

Write a comment...

3 **What name would you choose for a baby girl or a baby boy?**

## GRAMMAR

1 **Match each highlighted verb phrase in the article with a tense.**

*We brought – simple past*

2 **Write the negative form for each sentence and name the tense.**

a I like rock music.
*I don't like rock music. (simple present)*
b I'm reading a good book right now.
c I'm going to have some coffee after class.
d I went out last night.
e I've been to Peru.
f I can play the piano.

**Check (✓) the affirmative or negative sentences which are true for you.**

a *I like rock music.* ✓*/ I don't like rock music.*

3 **Write the question form for each sentence and the short answers *Yes* and *No*. Ask your partner the questions.**

a *Do you like rock music? Yes, I do. / No, I don't.*

**Tenses and auxiliary verbs**

**Simple present:** *do/does*
**Present progressive:** *am/are/is*
**Present perfect:** *have/has*
**Simple past:** *did*
**Future *(be) going to*:** *am/are/is*

## PRONUNCIATION

1 ▶ 1.04 **Listen and repeat the vowel sounds: /u/, /i/, /ɑ/, /ɜr/, /ɔ/.**

2 ▶ 1.05 **Listen and repeat the names in the table. Then label each group (a-e) with the correct vowel sound (/u/, /i/, /ɑ/, /ɜr/, /ɔ/).**

| a /u/ | b _____ | c _____ | d _____ | e _____ |
|---|---|---|---|---|
| June | Bert | Charles | Eve | Dawn |
| Luke | Pearl | Robert | Dean | Shaun |
| Sue | Kurt | Holly | Pete | Paul |

## LISTENING

1 ▶ 1.06 **How well can you remember names? Study the pictures of nine people below and listen to their names. Don't write them down.**

1

2

3

4

5

6

7

8

9

2 **Listen again and check. Who remembered the most names? Do you have any special techniques for remembering names?**

*I try to repeat the name in my head.*

## VOCABULARY

1 **Look at the pictures above. Complete the descriptions of each picture with the correct name and number.**

a *Toby (5)* has a shaved head. He's very good-looking.
b ____________ has short, straight hair with blond highlights.
c ____________ has dark hair and green eyes.
d ____________ has short, gray hair.
e ____________ has dark brown eyes and long hair.
f ____________ has long, blonde hair. She's very cute.
g ____________ has long, red hair. She has a beautiful smile.
h ____________ has dark, curly hair.
i ____________ has gray hair and a gray beard

▶ 1.07 **Listen, check, and repeat.**

2 **Complete the table with words and phrases from Exercise 1.**

| Hair length | Hair color | Hair style | Eyes | Opinion | Other |
|---|---|---|---|---|---|
| *a shaved head* | *dark* | *straight* | *green* | *very good-looking* | *a beard* |
| | | | | | |
| | | | | | |

3 ▶ 1.08 **Listen and repeat the words in the box. Then add them to the table in Exercise 2.**

a beard   beautiful   blue   fair   handsome   a mustache   a tattoo   wavy

4 **Pairwork Student A: page i   Student B: page iii**

## SPEAKING

1 **Work with a partner. Describe people in the class and guess their identity.**

She has long, straight hair and brown eyes. She has gold earrings.

Maria?

Yes, that's right. / No, that's wrong.

2 **Write short descriptions of three people you know. Tell your partner about them.**

## READING

1 **Read this top five. Match the headings (a-d) with the appropriate screen.**

- a ~~Looks like ...~~
- b How do you spell it?
- c Draw a picture!
- d Repeat!
- e Ask!

### TOP FIVE FUN: 5 Ways To Remember A Name

**No. 5** [a]

When you hear a name for the first time, try to make connections with the person in front of you. Who or what do they look like? Does Jo look like a doctor? Does Lola look like a lion? Is Sid a bit like a snake? Whatever the connection, it's going to help you. Next time you see Lola, you are going to think lion and then … "Ah, Lola the lion."

**No. 4** [ ]

A good plan is to repeat the person's name. Over and over and over again. Say it in your head, and then out loud. Say it right after you've been introduced to the person. Use the person's name in conversation. "Great to meet you, Mary," or "Mary, good to see you." Don't say it too much, of course.

**No. 3** [ ]

Ask the person you have just met to spell his/her name. As they spell it out (M-A-R…), visualize the letters in your mind. Or imagine you are writing the letters down. This is going to help you remember the name. Of course, if the person's name is Bob or Jo, you might want to try another method …You can also try to imagine the person's name written across his/her forehead. A big sign on their face!

**No. 2** [ ]

Another way to remember a name is to draw a picture in your mind. What does Bea sound like? Yes, a bee. So, in your mind, start drawing a big bumblebee. What does Lily remind you of? Of course. A flower! Draw a flower in your mind …

**No. 1** [ ]

If everything fails, then don't be afraid to give up … and just ask. It's much better to be honest and tell the person you have forgotten. It's much more embarrassing to get someone's name wrong. So, deep breath, and … "I'm so sorry, but what's your name again?"

2 **Discuss these questions with a partner.**

- a Which of these techniques have you used for remembering names?
- b Which of these techniques could help you remember new English words?
- c What other ways can you think of to help remember and learn new English words?

## GRAMMAR

1 **Look at the words and phrases in the box. Write N for nouns or noun phrases and A for adjectives or adjective phrases.**

[A] friendly [N] a banker [ ] intelligent [ ] shy
[ ] a doctor [ ] very young [ ] middle-aged [ ] stressed
[ ] about sixty [ ] Mexican [ ] a waiter [ ] a student
[ ] a retired police officer [ ] rich

**look(s)/look(s) like**

*look(s)* + adjective:
You **look** tired.

*look(s) like* + noun:
She **looks like** a student.

**What type of word do you use after *look(s)*? What type of word do you use after *look(s) like*?**

2 **Write a sentence to describe each person in the nine pictures on page 10. Leave a space for the name.**

_______________ *looks about fifty and pretty friendly. He looks like a banker.*

**Ask your partner to complete each sentence with the correct name.**

## READING

1 **Which of the following language learning tips do you follow? Tell a partner.**

- a Read as much as possible.
- b Speak as much as you can in class.
- c Buy a good dictionary.
- d Have a good reason for learning English.
- e Write down and review new language.
- f Watch English movies or TV shows.
- g Visit English-speaking countries.

2 **Read the Q&A with an English expert, Dr. Sally Haines. Which of the tips from Exercise 1 does she mention?**

# Today's Q&A:

Q&A: **Dr. Sally Haines** is a best-selling author and an associate professor of English.

## Dr. Sally Haines

**What's your best tip for language learners?**
There's a lot of advice for learners, but it can be confusing. So, I try to keep it very simple. For just about everyone, learning a language is about communication – so my best tip is very easy. Speak!

**When did you last study a language?**
I try to study a new language every year. This helps me understand what it's like to be a language learner. What does a language learner need? I also try to visit the country where they speak the language. This is something I recommend to everyone learning a language.

**Where do you go when you visit a new country?**
I always visit social places – cafés, restaurants, hotels, bars – and practice my new language. It's not always perfect, but it's great to be in a real-life situation and try to communicate.

**What do you enjoy about working with language learners?**
There is so much I enjoy. It's great to see my learners growing in confidence. And I love it when learners continue to learn English outside of class when they watch English movies or TV shows. Also, using a dictionary is very important.

**What kind of English dictionary do you recommend?**
Any! It doesn't matter if its print or digital, a dictionary is a very valuable tool for an English learner. To be an advanced learner, you need to learn over 5,000 words – that's why a dictionary is so useful.

**What other language learning tips can you think of? Write a list and compare with a partner.**

## SPEAKING

1 **Replace the highlighted words and phrases to make five new questions to ask a partner. Use the suggestions or your own ideas.**

- a What do you enjoy doing in class? (watching on TV / reading / doing in your free time)
- b When did you last read a book in English? (go dancing / buy a DVD / drink fruit juice)
- c Where do you write down new vocabulary? (go on vacation / do your shopping / have lunch)
- d What's your memory like? (house / city or town / family)
- e What kind of dictionary do you have? (computer / car / job)

2 **Ask your partner your questions from Exercise 1. What is the most interesting thing you've learned about your partner?**

## GRAMMAR

**1 Look at the table and match the questions (a–d) with the correct answers (1–4).**

| | | | |
|---|---|---|---|
| a | What are the blue words? — 2 | 1 | (auxiliary) verb + subject |
| b | What are the red words? | 2 | subjects |
| c | What is the word order for statements? | 3 | auxiliary verbs |
| d | What is the word order for questions? | 4 | subject + (auxiliary) verb |

**Question forms**

**Is** she hungry?
**Have** they arrived?
**What** does "nephew" mean?

| Statements | | | Questions | | | |
|---|---|---|---|---|---|---|
| You | are | left-handed. | | Are | you | left-handed? |
| Your mother | can | speak English. | | Can | your mother | speak English? |
| You | have | been to Peru. | | Have | you | been to Peru? |
| Your name | means | "first child." | What | does | your name | mean? |

**Ask a partner the questions in the table.**

**2 If necessary, rewrite these sentences with *do*, *does*, or *did* to make correct questions.**

a You play the guitar? *Do you play the guitar?*
b You sleep well last night?
c Can you drive?
d Where your mother come from?
e Have you been to California?
f What's your favorite color?

**Ask your partner the questions.**

**3 Rewrite these questions in the correct order. (DON'T ask your partner the questions!)**

a you / are / old / How ? *How old are you?*
b in life after death / Do / believe / you ?
c do / much / earn / you / How ?
d you / ever / Have / broken the law ?
e political party / vote / Which / you / do / for ?
f you / many / boyfriends or girlfriends / How / had / have ?

**Work in small groups. Decide which questions it is OK to ask ...**

- in your English class.
- in your family.
- with your best friends.
- at work.
- never!

**4** **Grammar Extra 1** page v. **Read the explanation and do the exercises.**

## SPEAKING: ANECDOTE

**1** 1.09 **Listen to Brad talking about somebody who is important to him. Underline the answers he gives.**

| | | |
|---|---|---|
| a | What's this person's name? | John Carter / Carl Johnson. |
| b | When did you meet him? | At college / When we were five years old. |
| c | Where does he live? | Near San Diego / In Los Angeles. |
| d | What does he do? | He's a teacher / a doctor. |
| e | How often do you see him? | Every weekend / In the summer. |
| f | Why is he important to you? | We have the same interests / He knows me so well. |
| g | What are his best qualities? | He's a really good listener / He's very funny. |
| h | What don't you like about him? | He's always late / too busy. |
| i | When did you last see him? | On my birthday / Last weekend. |

**2 You're going to tell your partner about a person who is important to you.**

- Ask yourself the questions in Exercise 1.
- Think about *what* to say and *how* to say it.
- Tell your partner about a person who is important to you.

## LANGUAGE FOR LIFE

1 1.10 **Listen to a conversation between two friends (Adam and Beth) discussing the weekend. Match the conversation with picture 1 or picture 2.**

Picture 1

Picture 2

2 1.11 **Listen to another version of the conversation. Does Beth sound more interested this time?**

3 1.12 **Listen and repeat the expressions Beth uses to show that she's interested.**

a Really?
b Do they?
c That sounds interesting.
d That sounds great.
e Wow! That's great.
f I've never heard of it.
g Oh, no! That's terrible.

Adam: Did you have a good weekend?
Beth: Not bad. How about you?
Adam: I had a really good dinner on Saturday night.
Beth: 1 Really?
Adam: Yes, we went to a new place in town – Edamame.
Beth: 2 ______
Adam: They have a Japanese chef from Tokyo.
Beth: 3 ______
Adam: And the food is fantastic – they make their own sushi.
Beth: 4 ______
Adam: Yes. It's the best sushi I've ever tasted.
Beth: 5 ______
Adam: And it wasn't expensive. We had appetizers, an entrée, dessert, and coffee, and it only cost $25 each.
Beth: 6 ______
Adam: I know. Unfortunately, when we got back to the car, we had a parking ticket.
Beth: 7 ______

4 **Complete the conversation with the expressions from Exercise 3. Check your answers and practice the conversation.**

5 **Work with a partner. Write a conversation about your last weekend. Include as many of the expressions as possible.**

### LIFE SKILLS: Cultural Awareness
**What's in a Name?**

1 **Work with a partner. Explain what your name means.**

2 **Look at these names, meanings, and nationalities. Which ones do you know?**

| | | | |
|---|---|---|---|
| a Rei | 1 "craftsman" | i Ethiopian |
| b Virat | 2 "warrior" | ii Swedish |
| c Abeda | 3 "brilliant" | iii Chinese |
| d Ana | 4 "bear" | iv Indian |
| e Bjorn | 5 "grace" | v French |
| f Fabrice | 6 "beautiful" | vi Mexican |
| g Hai | 7 "ocean" | vii Japanese |
| h Dieter | 8 "flower" | viii German |

1.13 **Listen and check your answers.**

3 **What English names do you know? Decide on the best names for these people.**

| Best name for ... | Name | Why? |
|---|---|---|
| an actor | | |
| a singer | | |
| a politician | | |
| a sports star | | |
| a writer | | |
| a celebrity | | |
| an English teacher | | |
| a rock band | | |

4 **Compare your name choices to your partner's.**

MACMILLAN LIFE SKILLS

# 1 Vocabulary Extra

## Family and other relationships

**1 Complete the table.**

| Male | Female | Definition |
|---|---|---|
| a grandson | *granddaughter* | Your children's children |
| b nephew | niece | Your brother's or __________'s children |
| c | grandmother | Your parents' parents |
| d great-grandfather | great-grandmother | Your grandparents' __________ |
| e uncle | aunt | Your parents' __________ and sister |
| f cousin | | Your aunt's or uncle's children |
| g brother-in-law | sister-in-law | Your wife's or husband's brother and __________ |
| h | mother-in-law | Your wife's or husband's father and mother |
| i stepfather | | Your mother's second husband or your father's second wife |
| j | half-sister | The children from your father's or mother's second relationship |
| k | ex-wife | The man or woman who you are divorced/separated from |
| l twin | | A brother or sister who was born at the same time as you |

**2 Work with a partner. Discuss these questions and compare your answers.**

a Who is your oldest relative?
Who is your youngest relative?

b Which side of the family is bigger:
your father's side or your mother's side?

c What are your neighbors like?
Do you know all your neighbors' names?

d How many close friends do you have?
Who is your best friend?

e Who are your favorite co-workers?
Are there any co-workers you don't like?

## Focus on names

**1 Underline the correct word.**

a My friends call / name me "Chip."

b I don't know the **meaning** / **sign** of my name.

c My parents **identified** / **named** me after my grandmother.

d I'm married, but I use my **maiden** / **feminine** name at work.

e My **letters** / **initials** are CJP.

f My **sign** / **signature** is very difficult to read.

**Check (✓) the sentences that are true for you.**

**2 Complete the form in as much detail as you can.**

| | |
|---|---|
| Title: __________ *(Mr./Mrs./Ms., etc.)* | Initials: __________ |
| First name: __________ *(Given name)* | Maiden name: __________ |
| Middle name(s): __________ *(Second name)* | Nickname: __________ |
| Last name: __________ *(Family name)* | Signature: __________ |
| Full name: __________ | |

# 2 The world

## VOCABULARY

1 **Look at the three pictures. Would you like to live in any of these places? Why? Why not? Discuss with a partner.**

Venice, Italy

La Bastide, France

Rio de Janeiro, Brazil

2 1.14 **Listen and repeat the words in the box. Which of these things can you find in the pictures?**

a beach a bridge a canal a castle a cathedral a church a fountain high-rise buildings a hill a library a mosque a museum the ocean a park a parking lot a shopping mall a square a statue

3 **How many of the things in Exercise 2 can you find near your school? Put them in the right order on this line.**

Nearest ⟷ Furthest away

- **Grammar:** Countable and uncountable nouns. *so/such*; *very/too*. Quantity expressions.
- **Vocabulary:** Places in a city. Adjectives. Countries, nationalities. Location. *like*.
- **Language for Life:** Saying where you are from

## LISTENING

**1** ▶ 1.15 **Listen to Paulo, Armelle, and Luigi talking about the three places in the pictures on page 16. Match each speaker with a picture. Who likes living where they live? Who doesn't?**

**2 Use the adjectives in the box to complete Paulo's, Armelle's, and Luigi's descriptions.**

| boring | clean | crowded | exciting |
|---|---|---|---|
| humid | polluted | romantic | small |

a ... a city that's so big and *exciting*
b ... it's too hot and _____
c ... the air is fresh and _____
d ... I find it so dull and _____
e ... it's such a _____ city.
f ... it gets very noisy and _____
g ... the canals are so dirty and _____
h ... my city is too _____ for all these people.

**Listen again and check your answers.**

## GRAMMAR & VOCABULARY

**1 Look at the sentences with *so* and *such a/an* in Exercise 2 in the Listening section. Complete the rules.**

a You use _____ + a negative or positive **adjective** for emphasis.
b You use _____ + a negative or positive **noun phrase** for emphasis.

> ***so/such***
>
> *so* + adjective
> It's **so** romantic.
>
> *such* + noun phrase
> It's **such** a romantic city.

**2 Use *so* and *such a/an* to complete the email. Is the person happy or unhappy?**

**To:** Ann Jones
**Subject:** Fantastic vacation

This is (1) *such* a beautiful place. We're (2) _____ lucky with our hotel. It's really close to downtown, and the staff is (3) _____ friendly. Our room is nice and clean, and we have (4) _____ fantastic view of the city. There are lots of good restaurants and bars, and they're (5) _____ cheap. It's (6) _____ interesting city. The museums and art galleries are great, and we're going to visit the royal palace tomorrow. It's (7) _____ exciting! We're having (8) _____ good time – we don't want to come home.

**3 Change the email in Exercise 2 to make it sound negative.**

*This is such an ugly place. We're ...*

**4 Look at the sentences with *very* and *too* in Exercise 2 in the Listening section. Complete the rules.**

a You use _____ + an **adjective** or an **adverb** to emphasize something.
b You use _____ + an **adjective** or an **adverb** to show that there is a problem: something is excessive or more than necessary.

> ***very/too***
>
> *very* + adjective/adverb
> We were **very** late (but we caught our train).
>
> *too* + adjective/adverb
> We were **too** late (so we missed our train).

**5 Complete the sentences with *very* or *too*.**

a My neighbors are _____ quiet. I never hear them.
b I can't walk to work. My office is _____ far from my house.
c I take the bus to work. It's _____ crowded, but I usually get a seat.
d It's _____ hot in the summer, but fortunately my office has air-conditioning.
e Time goes _____ quickly, and I never finish my work.
f I want to move into the city, but I can't because apartments are _____ expensive.

**Check (✓) any sentences that are true for you.**

## GRAMMAR

**1 Match each question with the most appropriate response.**

a How's the weather?
b What are the stores like?
c What are the people like?
d What's the architecture like?

1 It's a mixture of old and new.
2 They're really friendly.
3 They're too expensive.
4 It's hot and humid.

**Nouns**

**Countable**
a store / stores
a city / cities
a person / people

**Uncountable**
architecture
weather
traffic

**2 Complete the table with the nouns in the box.**

movie theater nightlife park person public transportation restaurant traffic

| Singular form | Plural form | Countable or uncountable? |
|---|---|---|
| *movie theater* | *movie theaters* | *countable* |
| *nightlife* | *–* | *uncountable* |

**Work with a partner. Discuss these questions.**

a How do you make plural forms of these nouns: *store*, *bus*, *church*, *city*, *country*, *leaf*?
b Which countable noun in the table has an irregular plural form?
c How do you make plural forms of these nouns: *man*, *woman*, *child*, *foot*, *tooth*?

**3 Work with your partner. Note down the names of two cities or villages you know well. Ask each other questions about the places you have noted down.**

*What's the nightlife like? It's great! There are lots of bars and clubs.*

## VOCABULARY & PRONUNCIATION

**1 Complete the following sets (A, B, and C). Underline the stressed syllable in each word.**

| A | | B | | C | |
|---|---|---|---|---|---|
| Country | Nationality | Country | Nationality | Country | Nationality |
| Cuba | C_____ | E_____ | Egyptian | China | C_____ |
| M_____ | Mexican | Italy | I_____ | V_____ | Vietnamese |
| B_____ | Brazilian | Hungary | H_____ | P_____ | Portuguese |
| Argentina | A_____ | C_____ | Canadian | Japan | J_____ |

1.16 **Listen, check, and repeat. What do you notice about the word stress in each set?**

**2 Write down six other countries you know and their nationalities. Mark the stress. Which countries would you most like to visit? Tell your partner.**

## SPEAKING

**1 Work in small groups. Do you agree with these statements?**

Argentinian beef is the best in the world.

Japanese cars are the best in the world

**2 Write similar statements which you all agree on. Combine a nationality with a noun from the box (or your own ideas).**

beer chocolate coffee colleges fashion food men movies nightlife perfume rock music soccer players women watches

Mexican music is the best in the world.

**Compare your statements with other groups.**

## READING & VOCABULARY

**1** **Read the reviews. Which of the places would you choose to stay in on vacation? Explain your choices to a partner.**

**resortsfinder.com**

reviews

SEARCH

pamelafox

**Milton Cape Town Lodge & Spa**

★★★

We had a good time at this hotel. We booked a deluxe room and it was fine for us. In a deluxe room, there are two beds, a TV, a desk and some chairs, and a couch. The bathroom has a very large bathtub and a great shower. It's too bad we only had a garden view, and no balcony, because there is a nice path through the trees to the beach. The city feels a million miles away, but all the top tourist attractions are only a 20-minute drive away.

5 likes 1d

lisa22

**Five Seasons Santa Barbara**

★★★★★

We're here on our honeymoon – and we got an upgrade to ... the presidential suite! Oh, wow, you have to see this place – it's bigger than our apartment! There's a hallway, a dining room, a small kitchen, TWO bedrooms and THREE bathrooms! It's so lovely – there are lots of lights and lamps. There are great views of the ocean from the balcony. I don't want to leave!

40 likes 2d

rachel101

**Sheriden Cancun**

★★★★

We're having a great time. We have a suite so the family can be together – there's a living room, which has a couch that turns into a double bed, and one bedroom. There is also a HUGE flat screen TV, so the boys are happy watching sports! We can enjoy eating at one of the six restaurants, and I can have a treatment at the spa. Nice place for a relaxing vacation!

85 likes 3w

tommydoe

**Turbury Gold Resort**

★

Please don't book a standard room. There is one small bed and no table. In the bathroom, there is only a sink and shower – the toilet is down the hallway! And some rooms don't have a window! I'm glad there is lots of nightlife around here, and big shopping malls, so we do not have to stay in the hotel.

102 likes 2m

**2** **Read and complete the table with words and phrases.**

| Hotel rooms | Rooms | Furniture |
|---|---|---|
| *deluxe room* | *bedroom* | *bed* |
| | | |
| | | |

**3** **Write a review about a hotel you have stayed in.**

## Reading

**1 Complete the following description of a country. Use the nouns in the box.**

| cars | cigarettes | coffee | hours | ~~meat~~ | noise | people | sleep | wine |
|---|---|---|---|---|---|---|---|---|

### Everything's wrong here!

They do everything wrong here! They eat way too much (1) *meat* and they eat it at 11:00 p.m. Yesterday we went out to dinner at 11:30 p.m. and we had trouble getting a table! At 1:00 a.m. we were still eating, and the restaurant was still half-full!

They smoke too many (2) ______. They drink lots of strong (3) ______, and a lot of (4) ______.

They spend too many (5) ______ in the sun and they certainly don't get enough (6) ______. One Saturday night we went to a disco at 2:00 a.m. and were surprised to see that there were only a few (7) ______ on the dance floor. Then the DJ arrived at 3:00 a.m. and the party began!

There are way too many (8) ______ in the cities, and there's too much (9) ______ everywhere! They do everything wrong here, but the quality of life is great, and people really know how to enjoy themselves. I don't want to go home!

**2 Which country do you think it is? Could it be your country? Why? Why not?**

## GRAMMAR

**1 Complete the headings for each category (A, B, C) with *countable* or *uncountable*.**

| A: With _____ nouns | B: With _____ nouns | C: With _____ and _____ nouns |
|---|---|---|
| How many? | How much? | not enough |
| (way) too many | (way) too much | a lot (of) |
| not many | not much | lots (of) |
| (only) a few | (only) a little | |

**Quantity expressions**

With countable nouns
How **many** people?
**too many**, **lots**, **a lot**, **not many**, **a few**, **not enough**

With uncountable nouns
How **much** traffic?
**too much**, **a lot**, **lots**, **not much**, **a little**, **not enough**

**2 Underline the correct quantity expression in each of these sentences.**

a I don't eat <u>much</u> / **many** bread.
b I eat **a few** / **lots of** fruit.
c I drink **way too much** / **way too many** coffee.
d I don't eat **much** / **enough** vegetables.
e I eat **a lot of** / **a little** cookies.
f I don't drink **enough** / **many** water

**Rewrite the sentences so that they are true for you.**

**3 Use the table to ask your partner questions about a city they like. Try to guess what city it is. Add your own nouns to make different questions.**

| | Nouns | | | | |
|---|---|---|---|---|---|
| Is there much | nightlife | pollution | traffic | public transportation | architecture |
| Are there many | beaches | bridges | parking lots | shopping malls | libraries |

*Is there much nightlife? Not much.* *Are there many beaches? Lots. Way too many!*

**4** Grammar Extra 2 page vii. Read the explanation and do the exercises.

## VOCABULARY

**1 Complete the labeling of the compass.**

**2 Match the descriptions (a–d) with the cities on the maps (1–4).**

- **a** It's central.
- **b** It's in the east.
- **c** It's on the west coast.
- **d** It's in the south-east.

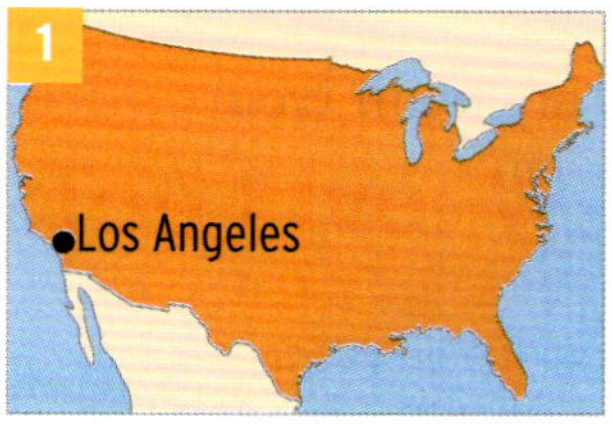


**The USA**

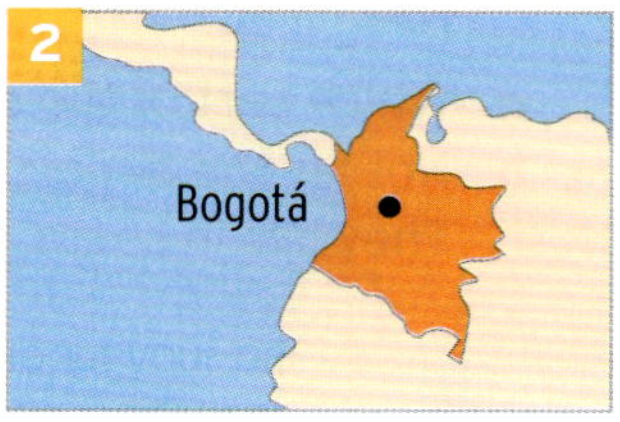


**Colombia**

**Great Britain**

**The USA**

**3** Pairwork: **Student A:** page i **Student B:** page iii

## SPEAKING: ANECDOTE

**1** 1.17 **Listen to Emma talking about the best place she has ever visited. Read the questions and check (✓) the ones she gives information about.**

- **a** Where is the place? ☑
- **b** When did you first go there? ☐
- **c** Were you on vacation? ☐
- **d** Who did you stay with? ☐
- **e** What was the room like? ☐
- **f** What did you do there? ☐
- **g** How many times have you visited the place? ☐
- **h** When was the last time? ☐
- **i** What do you like most about this place? ☐
- **j** Are there any things you don't like about this place? ☐
- **k** Would you like to live there? Why? Why not? ☐

**2 You're going to tell your partner about the best place you have ever visited.**

- Ask yourself the questions in Exercise 1.
- Think about *what* to say and *how* to say it.
- Tell your partner about the best place you have ever visited.

## LANGUAGE FOR LIFE

**1** 1.18 **Listen and read the conversation. What nationalities are Josh, Matt, and Erica?**

**Josh:** Matt, this is Erica.
**Matt:** Nice to meet you, Erica.
**Erica:** Nice to meet you, too.
**Matt:** You're not American, are you? Where are you from?

**Erica:** I live in New York, but I'm originally from England.
**Matt:** Oh, where exactly?
**Erica:** A small town just outside Manchester.
**Matt:** Manchester? Is that near London?
**Erica:** No, Manchester's in the north. And where are you from?
**Matt:** Well, I live in New York, too, but I'm actually from Los Angeles.
**Josh:** Hey, I'm from LA, too. Which part of the city are you from?
**Matt:** Santa Monica, not far from the airport.
**Josh:** Oh, great. My family lives in Hollywood.
**Erica:** Wow, really?
**Josh:** No, I'm kidding. They live in the south. Near South Beach.

**2** **Match each person with one of the maps below. Put a cross (✖) on each map to show exactly where each person comes from.**

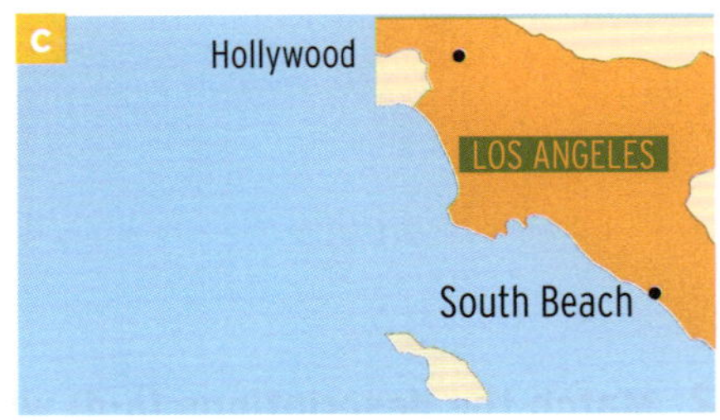


**3** **Complete the expressions with the words in parentheses.**

- **a** Where you from? (are) *Where are you from?*
- **b** I'm originally England. (from)
- **c** Where? (exactly)
- **d** A small town outside Manchester. (just)
- **e** Manchester's the north. (in)
- **f** I live in New York, but I'm from Los Angeles. (actually)
- **g** Which part of the city are from? (you)
- **h** Not far the airport. (from)
- **i** They live in south. (the)

1.19 **Listen, check, and repeat.**

**4** **Write a conversation between you and a partner about where you come from and where you live now.**

### LIFE SKILLS: Prioritizing

What to do ...?

**1** **Read the tweet. Work with a partner and complete the table with your own ideas about your city/town.**

> **Twitter**
> @ twitter
>
> Bob Denny @traveltopthrees 2m
> We're looking for new city recommendations for our new travel website – tell us the top three places to go, eat, and stay. Email me at bob@traveltopthrees.com

**Name of place:**

| Place to go | Cost (high/low) | Time (long/short) |
|---|---|---|
| | | |
| | | |
| | | |

**2** **Repeat the same exercise for places to eat and places to stay.**

MACMILLAN LIFE SKILLS

# 2 Vocabulary Extra

## Places

**1 Match the places in the picture with the words.**

| | | | |
|---|---|---|---|
| art gallery | 6 | museum | ___ |
| castle | ___ | parking lot | ___ |
| church | ___ | shopping mall | ___ |
| library | ___ | square | ___ |
| mosque | ___ | theater | ___ |

**2 Think about the last time you were in some of the different places in Exercise 1. Ask a partner.**

*When was the last time you were in an art gallery?*
*I'm not sure. Maybe when I went to Mexico City a few years ago.*

## Adjectives

**1 Look at the adjectives to describe cities. Decide which are positive and which are negative.**

*Positive: beautiful, ... Negative: boring, ...*

beautiful big boring crowded dirty
dull exciting expensive fabulous
interesting modern noisy polluted
romantic spectacular

**2 What are the five best adjectives to describe your town or city? Compare your answers with your partner.**

## Furniture

**1 Match the pictures with the words.**

| | | | | | | | |
|---|---|---|---|---|---|---|---|
| toilet | 4 | desk | ___ | shower | ___ | lamp | ___ |
| bathtub | ___ | couch | ___ | rug | ___ | sink | ___ |

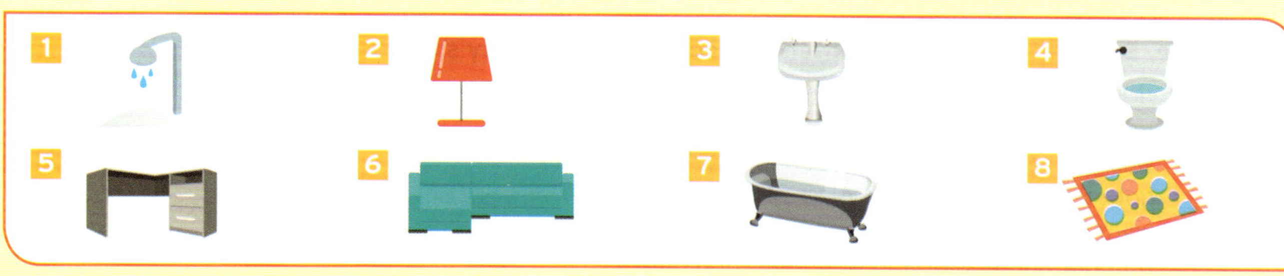


## Focus on *like*

**1 Match the uses of *like* (a-f) with the example sentences (1-6).**

| Uses of like | Examples |
|---|---|
| **a** *What* + *be* + somebody/something + *like* = asking for a description | **1** We like going out every Saturday night. I like cooking, but I don't like doing the dishes. |
| **b** verb + *like* = similar to somebody/something | **2** I really like Harry Potter. I've seen all the movies. I don't like her very much and she doesn't like me. |
| **c** *like* (+ *this/that*) = in this or that way | **3** She looks like her mother. They have the same eyes. It's plastic, but it feels like leather. |
| **d** *like* + noun/pronoun = somebody/something pleases you | **4** "What's your new teacher like?" "He's really nice." "What was Boston like?" "It was great." |
| **e** *like* + *ing* = enjoy an activity | **5** "Would you like a drink?" "Yes. I'd like a glass of cold water, please." |
| **f** *would like* + noun = want something | **6** Click on the "send" icon, like this. Cut the paper into squares. No, not like that, like this! |

**2 Write your own example sentence for each use of *like*.**

# 3 Love

## LISTENING

1 1.20 **Listen to Walt and Betty talking about their relationship and answer the questions.**

a When did they first meet?
b When did they get married to each other?

Walt fifty years ago

Betty fifty years ago

Betty and Walt now

2 **Write *He*, *She*, or *They* in these sentences about Walt and Betty's story.**

a They first met in Annapolis and dated for three months.
b _____ moved to different places and lost touch with each other.
c _____ was married to another person for forty-eight years.
d _____ got divorced after thirty years of marriage.
e _____ went to Annapolis with her grandson and visited all the old places.
f _____ thought about Walt and wanted to find him.
g _____ wrote a letter to the local newspaper.
h _____ had a cousin in Annapolis who told him about the letter.
i _____ met soon after that and moved in together.
j _____ got married – fifty years after they first met!

**Listen again and check your answers.**

## VOCABULARY & SPEAKING

1 **Complete the expressions in the sentences below with the words in the box.**

| get | have | live | lose | love |
|---|---|---|---|---|

a The best age to get married is twenty-five for women and twenty-seven for men.
b The main reason for getting married is to _____ children.
c A big difference in age isn't a problem for a couple if they are in _____.
d It's a good idea for a couple to _____ together for a few years before getting married.
e It doesn't matter if children _____ touch with one of their parents.

| I agree / don't agree, because ... |
|---|
| I slightly disagree ... |
| I am against ... |

2 **Work in small groups. Discuss the statements in Exercise 1. Use the expressions in the box.**

- **Grammar:** Simple past and past progressive. Adverbs of manner.
- **Vocabulary:** Relationship expressions. Narrative linkers. *ed/ing* adjectives; *get.*
- **Language for Life:** Things in common

## VOCABULARY

**1 Match each of the verb phrases in the box with an appropriate picture (a–d).**

flirt with somebody | have a crush on somebody | have a fight | move in together

a

b

c

d

**2 Put the stages of a relationship in a logical order (a–l). Add or take away stages if you think it's necessary.**

a You get married.
b You flirt with somebody.
c You call somebody.
d You have a crush on somebody.
e You move in together.
f You have children.
g You meet the parents.
h You date somebody.
i You have a fight.
j You kiss.
k You split up.
l You fall in love.

**Compare your ideas with a partner.**

## GRAMMAR

**Simple past**

He **went** to Annapolis.
He **didn't go** to Delaware.

**Did** he **go** to Chicago?
Yes, he **did**.
No, he **didn't**.

**1 Write the affirmative and negative simple past forms of the verbs in the box.**

be can get go have flirt kiss like meet move study want

*be – was/were, wasn't/weren't*

**2 Write true sentences – affirmative or negative – with the verbs in parentheses.**

a My mother and father (meet) at college.
b My grandparents (get) married in a church.
c I (have) a big breakfast this morning.
d I (go) skiing last winter.
e I (study) German at school.
f I (be) very busy yesterday.

**Make questions and ask your partner.**

*Did your mother and father meet at college? No, they didn't.*

**3** Grammar Extra 3, Part 1 **page ix. Read the explanation and do the exercises.**

## PRONUNCIATION

**1 Complete these irregular verb sets. Label the past forms in each group (1–3) with these sounds: /æ/, /e/, /ɔ/.**

1.21 **Listen, check, and repeat.**

| 1 Infinitive | Past: */e/* | 2 Infinitive | Past: ______ | 3 Infinitive | Past: ______ |
|---|---|---|---|---|---|
| keep | kept | begin | c ______ | bring | brought |
| mean | a *meant* | drink | d ______ | e ______ | bought |
| b ______ | met | ring | rang | catch | f ______ |

**2 Add the verbs in the box to the correct groups in the table in Exercise 1.**

fight read sing sleep swim teach

1.22 **Listen, check, and repeat.**

## LISTENING

**1 Read about a TV game show called *Get Personal* and answer these questions.**

a Who are the two people playing *Get Personal* tonight?
b How much is the prize money?
c How can they win?

### *Get Personal*

Game show *Get Personal* is hosted by Bobby Brown. In tonight's show, contestants Rosie and Dave try to win the $10,000 prize. The game is very simple. Bobby interviews Rosie and Dave in separate studios. He asks them the same questions about how they first met, and they have to give the same answers. Can they do it?

**Watch OTV at 8:30 tonight and find out.**

**2** 1.23 **Read the questions and answers in the table below. Listen and choose the answers (*a*, *b*, or *c*) that Rosie gives.**

| Questions | Rosie's answers | | Dave's answers |
|---|---|---|---|
| 1 How did you first meet? | a She was a nurse. He was a patient.<br>b She was a patient. He was a nurse.<br>c She was a doctor. He was a nurse. | | ✓ / ✖ |
| 2 What time of day was it? | a Early morning.<br>b Early afternoon.<br>c Early evening. | | ✓ / ✖ |
| 3 How was the weather? | a The sun was shining.<br>b It was raining.<br>c It was snowing. | | ✓ / ✖ |
| 4 What were you both wearing? | She was wearing …<br>a a white coat.<br>b a green uniform.<br>c a nightgown. | He was wearing …<br>a blue pajamas.<br>b green pajamas.<br>c a white coat. | ✓ / ✖ |
| 5 Who spoke first and what did they say? | a She said: "How are you feeling?"<br>b He said: "I'm going to throw up."<br>c He said: "I feel terrible." | | ✓ / ✖ |

**3** 1.24 **Listen to Dave answering the same questions. Circle the ✓ if he gives the same answer as Rosie. Circle the ✖ if he gives a different answer.**
**How many points did Rosie and Dave score out of five?**

**4 Think about your closest friend. How many of the questions from *Get Personal* could you answer? Discuss with a partner.**

## GRAMMAR

**1 Look at these extracts from Bobby Brown's interview with Rosie. Answer the questions (a–d) with *Simple past* or *Past progressive*.**

*I was working as a nurse, and Dave came into the hospital for an operation.*
*Yes, it was raining when I arrived at work.*
*What were you wearing when you saw each other for the first time?*

a What tense is used for the verbs *come*, *arrive*, and *see*? *Simple past.*
b What tense is used for the verbs *work*, *rain*, and *wear*?
c Which tense describes something that was in progress when another event happened?
d Which tense describes an event that happened at a particular moment in the past?

**Past progressive**

I **was**
You **were**
He **was**
She **was** **working**.
It **was**
We **were**
They **were**

**Were** you **working**?
Yes, I **was**.
No, I **wasn't**.

**2** Pairwork: **Student A:** i **Student B:** page iii

**3** 1.25 **Look at the pictures (1–5) and listen to the recordings. Work with a partner. Write sentences about Jake and Fiona to describe the five situations.**

1 *Jake was taking a shower when his cell phone rang.*

**4** Grammar Extra 3, Part 2 **page ix. Read the explanation and do the exercises.**

## READING

**1 Complete the story with past progressive or simple past verb forms. Predict the ending of the story.**

# BCB News

home news sport entertainment **lifestyle** search

19 June 6:45 p.m. share

### How we met: A Love of Horror!

"How I (1 meet) *met* my husband is a funny story.
Three years ago, he (2 tweet) ______ that he (3 move) ______ and he had lots of horror DVDs he wanted to give away. At the time, we (4 not follow) ______ each other on Twitter, but a friend showed me his tweet.
I am a huge horror movie fan, so I (5 agree) ______ to come and pick up the DVDs. They (6 wait) ______ on the front porch when I got to his house, but he wasn't at home.
I tweeted to say "thank you".
He (7 reply) ______ and asked me out for a coffee. He's a writer, so he said he (8 write) ______ a book and he wanted to interview me for it. I (9 meet) ______ him, and he asked me all sorts of questions about my business.
At the end of the meeting he then asked me if I would like to go out for dinner with him any other day. I had to laugh! I really thought he wanted to interview me and that was it. After we were seeing each other for a few months, I (10 ask) ______ him when he was planning to write the book ..."

1.26 **Listen and check your prediction.**

## READING

**1 Look at the pictures and complete the noun phrases with the words in the box.**

| bag | club | ~~paint~~ | party | scissors | mineral water |
|---|---|---|---|---|---|

a

a can of ___*paint*___

b

a dinner ____________

c

a pair of ____________

d

a night ____________

e

a plastic ____________

f

a bottle of ____________

**2 Complete the story with the noun phrases from Exercise 1.**

LESSONS IN LOVE:

# *A Pink House!*

Last year, Bill and Lisa were invited to a (1) *dinner party* to help celebrate their fiftieth wedding anniversary. That evening, as they walked back from the party, Lisa said something very surprising.

"I'm bored, Bill. Really bored. We do the same things over and over. Couldn't we do something crazy one day?"

At first, Bill was shocked and angry. When he got back home, he went out to the garden and stared at the plants unhappily. Then he drank a big (2) _____ of water. That night, Bill couldn't sleep. Why hadn't Lisa ever mentioned that she was bored?

The next morning, Bill had a plan.

"Okay, Lisa. Let's never be bored again!"

Next, he gave her a (3) ____ of scissors.

"Go upstairs. Any clothes you are bored of? Cut them up!"

After Lisa came down with a big grin, and an even bigger (4) _____ bag filled with cut up clothes, Bill led her to the shed.

"Okay, choose a (5) _____ of paint."

Lisa chose one that was pink. A week later, their boring white house was a beautiful bright pink!

One day, Bill and Lisa went to the airport, looked quickly at the departure board, chose a destination, and bought two tickets. They spent two happy weeks there!

At the end of August this year, Bill and Lisa celebrated their fifty-first wedding anniversary ... by going to a (6) ______ for the first time in decades. They danced all night!

1.27 **Listen and check your answers.**

**3 What do you think you can do to stop a life from getting boring? Discuss with a partner.**

## VOCABULARY & SPEAKING

**1** **Find and underline the time adverbials from the box in the blog post on page 28. Which adverbial is not in the text?**

| | | | | | |
|---|---|---|---|---|---|
| A week later | At first | At the end of August | One day | ~~Last year~~ | Next |
| After | That evening | That night | The next morning | Then | |

**List the time adverbials in the order in which they appear in the blog post.**

1 Last year
2 ______
3 ______
4 ______
5 ______
6 ______
7 ______
8 ______
9 ______
10 ______
11 ______

**2** **Use the time adverbials in Exercise 1 to retell the story to a partner. Don't look at the text on page 28.**

## GRAMMAR

**1** **Work with a partner. Complete the table with adverbs or adjectives from the story on page 28.**

| | Adjective | Adverb |
|---|---|---|
| a | happy | happily |
| b | ______ | surprisingly |
| c | ______ | angrily |
| d | quick | ______ |
| e | ______ | beautifully |
| f | unhappy | ______ |
| g | quiet | ______ |

**Answer these questions.**

a How do you make adverbs from most adjectives?
b How do you make adverbs from adjectives ending in *y*?
c What are the adverbs for the adjectives *good*, *early*, *late*?

**Adverbs of manner**

**Add *ly* to most adjectives:**
bad**ly**, careful**ly**, angr**ily**

**Exceptions:**
well, early, late, fast

**2** **Rewrite these sentences in the usual order.** subject + verb + object + adverb

a I / very quickly / eat / my lunch — I | eat my | lunch | very quickly.
b drive / my car / I / very slowly
c plan / my days / very carefully / I
d I / my money / spend / very intelligently
e play / I / tennis / very badly
f very regularly / clean / I / my house
g I / speak / very well / English

**How many sentences are true for you? Rewrite the sentences so that they are all true for you. Compare your sentences with your partner.**

## LANGUAGE FOR LIFE

**1** 1.28 **Listen to a conversation between a man (Tim) and a woman (Anna) on a train. Do they know each other?**

**2 Are these sentences true or false?**

a The man and woman are going to Atlanta.
b She's reading *Pride and Prejudice*.
c They both like Keira Knightley.
d They're both going to see Johnny Depp's new movie tomorrow night.
e They're both single.

**Listen again and check your answers.**

**3 Complete the expressions in the table using the phrases in the box.**

Me, too | Neither do I | Oh, I did | So am I | So do I

| | **Comment** | **Agree** | **Disagree** |
|---|---|---|---|
| a | I didn't like the movie. | Neither did I. / Me, neither. | (1) ________ . |
| b | I really like Keira Knightley. | (2) ________ . / Me, too. | Oh, I don't. |
| c | I think she's really good. | So do I. / (3) ________ . | Oh, I don't. |
| d | I'm going to see Johnny Depp's new movie. | (4) ________ . / Me, too. | Oh, I'm not. |
| e | I don't know what time it starts. | (5) ________ . / Me, neither. | Oh, I do. |

1.29 **Listen, check, and repeat the expressions.**

**4 Write true comments using these sentence beginnings.**

I think ... | I don't like ... | I'm not going ... | Last weekend, I didn't ...
I really like ... | I'm going ... | Yesterday evening, I ...

## LIFE SKILLS: Decision-making

### A Perfect Date

**1** 1.30 **Listen and complete the dating profile for each person.**

**2 What would be the perfect date for the people in Exercise 1? Discuss and choose, giving your reasons.**

a French restaurant | a soccer game | nightclub | a movie festival | the opera

Petra & Stevie ______________________________
Petra & Donny ______________________________

**3 What would be your perfect date? Why? Tell your partner.**

My perfect date would be going to the theater because ...

a

**Petra**
Age: _____
Job: designer
Character: _____
Likes: French movies
Dislikes: _____

b

**Stevie**
Age: 24
Job: _____
Character: loud and confident
Likes: _____
Dislikes: _____

c

**Donny**
Age: _____
Job: company owner
Character: _____
Likes: new places
Dislikes: _____

MACMILLAN LIFE SKILLS

# 3 Vocabulary Extra

## Adjectives ending in *ed* or *ing*

**1 Match the pictures with the pairs of adjectives.**

| | | | |
|---|---|---|---|
| annoyed / annoying | 5 | excited / exciting | ___ |
| bored / boring | ___ | frightened / frightening | ___ |
| confused / confusing | ___ | interested / interesting | ___ |
| depressed / depressing | ___ | surprised / surprising | ___ |
| embarrassed / embarrassing | ___ | tired / tiring | ___ |

1 
2 
3 
4 
5 
6 
7 
8 
9 

10 

**2 Underline the correct adjective.**

1 The students are **boring / bored**.
2 The teacher is **interesting / interested**.
3 The score is **depressing / depressed**.
4 The daughter is **embarrassing / embarrassed**.
5 The dog is **annoying / annoyed**.
6 The people are **frightening / frightened**.
7 The boy is **surprising / surprised**.
8 The race is **exciting / excited**.
9 The man is **tiring / tired**.
10 The map is **confusing / confused**.

## Focus on *get*

**1 Match the uses of *get* (a–e) with the examples (1–5).**

| | Some uses of *get* | | Examples |
|---|---|---|---|
| a | *get* + adjective = become | 1 | Did you get my text message?<br>I got my new shoes on sale.<br>She's trying to get a new job. |
| b | phrasal verbs with *get* | 2 | It doesn't get dark till 10:00 p.m. in the summer.<br>He's getting better at English.<br>This room never gets warm enough. |
| c | *get* + noun = buy, obtain, or receive | 3 | What time do you get to work?<br>I got home very late last night.<br>We'll never get there in time. |
| d | *get* = arrive | 4 | It's time to get moving.<br>They got married in a hotel.<br>I always have breakfast before I get dressed. |
| e | Expressions with *get*<br>+ present/past participle | 5 | He never gets up before 10:00 a.m.<br>We don't get along with our neighbors.<br>The whole family gets together at Thanksgiving. |

**2 Use a dictionary. Find and write your own example sentence for each use of *get*.**

# Review A

## GRAMMAR

Grammar Extra pages v-x.

**1 Complete the questions with the correct auxiliaries and name the tenses.**

am/is/are do/does did have/has

a ___Have___ you ever been to Chicago?
*Present perfect*
b ________ you like jazz?
c Where ________ you go on vacation last year?
d Where ________ you going to go on vacation this year?
e Where ________ you living now?
f ________ you ever seen Machu Picchu?
g What ________ you do for a living?

**Ask and answer the questions with a partner.**

**2 Underline the correct words.**

Di: Rome is (**1**) **<u>such a</u>** / **so** great city, isn't it?
Jo: I don't like it. It's (**2**) **too** / **very** hot for me.
Di: The weather's perfect. It's really (**3**) **too** / **very** nice.
Jo: But the streets are (**4**) **such a** / **so** crowded.
Di: Yes, but it's (**5**) **such a** / **so** wonderful experience.
Jo: Well, I'm not enjoying it. It's (**6**) **too** / **very** noisy!
Di: Jo, don't be (**7**) **such a** / **so** boring. We're in a (**8**) **too** / **very** beautiful place. Come on, smile. ...

**3 Write one verb in the simple past and the other in the past progressive for each sentence.**

a I (work) ___was working___ in Ohio when I (meet) ___met___ Tony for the first time.
b It (rain) ____________ when Sara (got) ____________ home.
c We (have) ____________ lunch when you (call) ____________ .
d You (talk) ____________ when I (come) ____________ in.
e Joe (cook) ____________ when he (cut) ____________ his finger.
f Dave and Becky (watch) ____________ TV when the baby (wake) ____________ up.

**4 Change the adjectives in the box into adverbs and use them to complete the sentences.**

careful early good quiet regular

a I wash my car ___regularly___ - every Saturday.
b I don't cook very ___________ - everyone hates my food!
c I usually speak very ___________ - no one can hear me!
d I always get up ___________ - at 6:00 a.m.
e I do my work ___________ - I never make mistakes!

**Check (✓) the sentences that are true for you.**
**Compare with your partner.**

**5 Find the mistake! Cross out the incorrect sentence.**

1 a ~~What means your name?~~
b What does your name mean?
2 a Did they been to Miami?
b Have they ever been to Miami?
3 a What was Florida like?
b How was Florida like?
4 a We eat way too much chocolate.
b We eat way too many chocolate.
5 a You eat your food very slowly.
b You eat very slowly your food.
6 a They speak Spanish very good.
b They speak Spanish very well.

## VOCABULARY

**1 Complete the text about Gary and his family with the words in the box.**

brother-in-law daughter half-brother half-sister nephew niece ~~stepfather~~ stepmother uncle

Hi, I'm Gary, and this is my family. My dad, Bill, and my mom, Lisa, are divorced. Dad is single, but Mom remarried. Her husband - my (**1**) *stepfather* - is named Phil. Mom and Phil have two children, Jack and Cathy - my (**2**) ____________ and my (**3**) ____________. Phil and his ex-wife, Eva, have a (**4**) ____________, Debra. My mom is Debra's (**5**) ____________. My sister's name is Ann. She's married to Ted - (**6**) my ____________. They have two children. Brennah is my (**7**) ____________ and Brendan is my (**8**) ____________, and, of course, I'm their favorite (**9**) ____________. They're great children.

**2 Complete the names of places you might find in a city.**

- **a** _a_rt g_a_llery
- **b** br__dg__
- **c** c__n__l
- **d** p__rk__ng l__t
- **e** c__stl__
- **f** f__ __nt__ __n
- **g** l__br__ry
- **h** m__s__ __m
- **i** p__rk
- **j** sh__pp__ng m__ll

**3 Write an adjective from the box next to each definition.**

beautiful ~~crowded~~ dull expensive polluted romantic spectacular

- **a** full of people *crowded*
- **b** too much smoke/traffic
- **c** not interesting
- **d** ideal for lovers
- **e** costs a lot of money
- **f** very good-looking
- **g** dramatic and exciting

**4 Look at the map of Australia and write sentences about the places using the words in the box.**

central east north north-east south south-east south-west

*Darwin is in the north. Cairns is in ...*

## PRONUNCIATION

**1 Look at some words from Units 1–3. Say the words and add them to the table.**

~~annoyed~~ ~~beautiful~~ ~~cathedral~~ ~~central~~ Chinese chocolate cousin Cuba dessert Egyptian extremely finally granddaughter surprised together uniform

| | | | |
|---|---|---|---|
| **A** •● *annoyed* | | | |
| **B** ●• *central* | | | |
| **C** ●•• *beautiful* | | | |
| **D** •●• *cathedral* | | | |

**2 Underline the stressed syllable in each word.**

1.31 **Listen, check, and repeat.**

## READING & LISTENING

**1** 1.32 **Read the descriptions of two friendships and answer the questions.**

a How did these best friends meet?
b How often do they see each other?

# Who's your BFF?

*We ask celebrities about their BFF (Best Friend Forever!). This week, Josh, from the reality TV show The Adventurer, and Sally, anchor on WCBS Evening News.*

## Josh

(reality TV star)

**Who's your BFF?**

My best friend is Thomas Stevens. Or Tommy, as I call him. He doesn't like it, but I think it suits him …

**How did you meet?**

We met at elementary school. Tom is quite small and was getting bullied a little. I stepped in and we became good friends. Tom had this amazing collection of comics, so after class we sat and read these comics for hours and hours! We liked the same things in high school and hung out all the time. But Tom went to college on the other side of the country and so we didn't see each other for about five years. But then he saw me on TV and got in contact on social media. Now, we're big friends again! It's great!

**How often do you see each other?**

We talk a lot on social media. He makes jokes about the show, and we gossip about the other stars. He's now back in California, so we meet up a couple of times a month.

## Sally

(news anchor)

**Who's your BFF?**

My best friend is Phoebe. She's so brave and kind!

**How did you meet?**

Before I was a news anchor, I was a reporter for the local newspaper. I met Phoebe because I was the reporter covering her story. She has had cancer three times, but even when she was sick, she was raising money for the local hospital. I did a story and then asked her how I could help – and that's when we became friends. Thankfully, she's healthy right now, but she's still raising money – and she's just finished a marathon!

**How often do you see each other?**

We always speak on the phone – I know, we're like teenagers! But she's always great to talk to, and she inspires me to be better every day. We meet up on the weekend and go shopping or just hang out in the local park chatting.

**2 Read the descriptions again. Are these statements true or false? Correct the false statements.**

a Josh and Tom met at college. *False*
b Josh thinks Tom is very serious.
c Josh and Tom live in California.
d Sally thinks Phoebe is brave and inspiring.
e Sally and Phoebe never talk on the phone.
f Sally and Phoebe often hang out at the office.

**3** 1.33 **Listen to the conversation between Carol and Jennifer. What nationality is Matt?**

**Listen again and underline the correct information.**

a Where Jennifer and Matt met: **(1) At school / At college.**
b When they met: **(2) Five years ago / Ten years ago.**
c First impression: **(3) She didn't like him / She thought he was very interesting.**
d Things they really like doing together: **(4) Windsurfing / Scuba diving.**

**4 Listen again and answer the questions.**

a What did Jennifer and Matt do at the beach?
b Where did Matt go after college?
c Why did they go to Egypt?
d Has Jennifer been to Australia?
e When did Matt come back to the USA?
f Where are Jennifer and Matt going to travel to next?

## WRITING & SPEAKING

**1 Work with a partner. Match the questions (a–e) with the answers in note form (1–5).**

a What's your best friend's name? 3
b Where and when did you meet him/her?
c What was your first impression of him/her?
d What do you like about him/her?
e What do you like doing together?

1. relaxed, good listener, funny
2. high school – 1st day
3. Adriana Costa
4. theater, museums, shopping
5. she knew everybody

**2 Match the parts of the text below to the questions (a–e) in Exercise 1.**

**3 How did you meet your best friend? Write answers in note form to the questions in Exercise 1.**

# How I met my best friend

[ ] We met on the first day of high school. I was very shy, and I felt nervous on my first day.

[ ] We are very different. I'm pretty serious. But Adriana is a very relaxed person, and she's a really good listener. And she's the funniest person I've ever met. We laugh all the time.

[a] My best friend is Adriana Costa.

[ ] We do everything together! We both like the theater and art. We visit museums and we love shopping!

[ ] Adriana knew everybody, and everybody liked her. I liked her too, but I thought she was too cool, and I was too shy. But she still liked me! I was sitting alone in the classroom when she sat down next to me. She was very nice to me, and we became good friends.

**4 Tell your partner about how you met your best friend.**

**5 Write about how you met your best friend. Give longer answers to the questions in Exercise 1.**

# 4 Shopping

## SPEAKING

**Work in small groups. Discuss the questions.**

a When do you give gifts?
b What's the best gift you've ever given or received?
c Which is easier: buying gifts for men or buying gifts for women?

## READING

**1 Read the tweets and answer the questions.**

a How many men forgot to buy a gift?
b Which gift came wrapped?
c Who received instant coffee?
d Which gift was the most expensive?

### The Worst Gifts ... Ever!

Follow

Simple Flowers
@simpleflowers 2h

So it's Valentine's Day again ... let us know the worst gifts you've ever received using the hashtag #worstgiftever.

7 16 9

Rosa Gray @rosashopping 1h
I never get a gift, good or bad, because my boyfriend always forgets! #worstgiftever

Jill Stevens @jillstevens20 1h
I usually get a houseplant from my husband. And the plant never survives more than about a month. Thanks, hon! #worstgiftever

Dave Iztkoff @itzkoffd 1h
I hardly ever get any gifts, but once at college I got a box of chocolates from a girlfriend. She even wrapped them using silver paper ... I guess a few were missing. #worstgiftever

Carrie Travis @carrietravis 42m
My boyfriend rarely remembers when Valentine's Day is. One year, I got some flowers – on *January*14th #worstgiftever

Phil Plumber @thephilplumber 36m
She normally buys something at the last minute from the corner store – last year it was a jar of instant coffee and a bunch of grapes. I still love her, though! #worstgiftever

Fred Jarvis @jfred33 4m
We sometimes buy each other expensive gifts. One year I got her some silver jewelry. She got me a gold watch. We don't buy expensive gifts these days. #worstgiftever

Gina Ingall @ginaingall 30s
My boyfriend often forgot to buy me a gift on Valentine's Day. We ended up marrying on Valentine's Day and now he forgets his wedding anniversary as well! #worstgiftever

**2 Who do you think is the worst at buying Valentine's Day gifts? Discuss with a partner.**

- **Grammar:** Adverbs of frequency. Verbs patterns. Simple present and present progressive.
- **Vocabulary:** Collocations: *a bunch of ... a box of ...*, etc. Clothes and accessories.
- **Language for Life:** In a clothing store

## VOCABULARY

**1 Match words from column A with words from column B to make collocations.**

| A | B |
|---|---|
| **a** a bunch of | **1** socks / scissors / jeans |
| **b** a box of | **2** cake / furniture / wood |
| **c** a pair of | **3** sweets / gum |
| **d** a pack of | **4** flowers / grapes / keys |
| **e** a piece of | **5** water / perfume / juice |
| **f** a bottle of | **6** beans / paint / tomatoes |
| **g** a jar of | **7** chocolates / matches / tissues |
| **h** a can of | **8** jam / instant coffee / mayonnaise |

**2 Work with a partner. Discuss the questions about the things in Exercise 1.**

- Have you ever given or received any of these things as a gift?
- Which things are common gifts in your country?

## PRONUNCIATION

**1** 1.34 **Listen and repeat the plural forms in the table.**

| /s/, /z/, or /ɪz/ ? | | Example |
|---|---|---|
| A: | /s/ after /p/, /k/, /f/, /t/, /θ/ | *cakes, chips, suits* |
| B: | /z/ after /b/, /g/, /v/, /d/, /ð/, /l/, /m/, /n/, /ŋ/, /r/, and all vowel sounds | *clothes, rings, views* |
| C: | /ɪz/ after /s/, /z/, /ʃ/, /tʃ/, /dʒ/ | *beaches, places, stages* |

**2 Add the plural forms of these nouns to the appropriate line in the table in Exercise 1.**

bar /bar/ bridge /brɪdʒ/ bunch /bʌntʃ/ grape /greɪp/ key /ki/
piece /pis/ pot /pɑt/ sock /sɑk/ tie /taɪ/

1.35 **Listen, check, and repeat.**

## GRAMMAR

**1 Look at the highlighted examples of adverbs of frequency used in the tweets on page 32. Are these sentences true or false?**

**a** Adverbs of frequency come before the main part of the verb, but after auxiliary verbs.

**b** Adverbs of frequency come after the verb *be*.

**2 How well do you know the person sitting next to you? Add an adverb of frequency to these sentences to make them true. Write affirmative or negative sentences.**

**a** He/She spends more than $25 on a gift.
*She rarely spends more than $25 on a gift.*

**b** He/She is positive about life.

**c** He/She goes out on the weekend.

**d** He/She is late for appointments.

**e** He/She has lunch at home during the week.

**Check your sentences with your partner. How many are true? How similar or different are you?**

**Adverbs of frequency**

100% always
usually
normally
often
sometimes
occasionally
rarely
hardly ever
0% never

**adverb** before main verb
We don't **usually** drive.
*be* before **adverb**
I'm **always** tired.

## SPEAKING: ANECDOTE

1 1.36 **Listen to Eddie talking about the last time he bought somebody a gift. Underline the answers he gives.**

a Who was the gift for? My **friend** / **sister**.
b What was the occasion? Her **birthday** / **wedding anniversary**.
c Where did you go shopping for the gift? **To the mall** / **On the internet**.
d Did you know what you were going to buy? **Yes, I did** / **No, I didn't**.
e What did you buy in the end? **Jewelry** / **A foot spa**.
f How much did you spend? About **$50** / **$15**.
g Did you buy a card too? **Yes, I did** / **No, I didn't**.
h Did the person like the gift? **Yes, she did** / **No, she didn't**.
i Was it the kind of gift you would like to receive? **Yes, it was** / **No, it wasn't**.

2 **You're going to tell your partner about the last time you bought somebody a gift.**

- Ask yourself the questions in Exercise 1.
- Think about *what* to say and *how* to say it.
- Tell your partner about the last time you bought someone a gift.

## GRAMMAR & VOCABULARY

1 **Look at these two sentences and answer the questions.**

Eddie bought a foot spa for his sister.
Eddie bought his sister a foot spa.

a Do the sentences mean the same thing?
b What color is the direct object in each sentence?
c What color is the indirect object in each sentence?

**Verbs patterns 1**

**Verbs with two objects**
*buy* somebody something
*send* somebody something
*give* somebody something

***somebody*** = indirect object

***something*** = direct object

2 **Complete the table to show two ways of saying the same thing.**

| subject + verb + thing + *to/for* + person | subject + verb + person + thing |
|---|---|
| a I never lend my car to anybody. | I never lend anybody my car. |
| b My friends send lots of texts to me. | ______________________ |
| c I sometimes buy flowers for my mom. | ______________________ |

**Check (✓) the sentences that are true for you.**

3 **Insert the indirect object in parentheses to complete the questions.**

When was the last time ...
a you bought gifts? (your family)
*you bought your family gifts?*
b you made coffee? (somebody)
c your bank sent a letter? (you)
d you gave a ride? (somebody)
e you lent some money? (your best friend)
f a friend told a joke? (you)

**Ask your partner the questions.**

4 **Grammar Extra 4, Part 1** page xi. Read the explanation and do the exercises.

## SPEAKING

**1 Complete these statements with *Men or Women* as you think appropriate.**

- **a** _____ can't stand shopping for clothes.
- **b** _____ don't mind spending hours and hours shopping for clothes.
- **c** _____ spend a lot of time going from store to store, comparing prices and quality.
- **d** _____ never forget to look at the price tag before they buy.
- **e** _____ only agree to go shopping when they really need to buy something.
- **f** _____ like going to the dentist more than going shopping.

**2 Discuss your answers with a partner. Which statements in Exercise 1 are true for you?**

## GRAMMAR

**1 Complete these interviews with two men about shopping. Use the *ing* form or the *to*-infinitive.**

**Verb patterns 2**

**Verbs + *ing* form**
avoid can't stand
don't mind enjoy hate
like love spend time

I can't stand **shopping**.

**Verbs + *to*-infinitive**
agree can't afford
choose decide forget
manage need refuse
want would like

I can't afford **to buy** it.

| Questions | Conor, 26, writer | Jim, 32, designer |
|---|---|---|
| **Question 1** Do you mind (1 go) *going* to the shopping mall? | Not really. But after about an hour, I want (2 go) _______ home. | Actually, I can't stand (3 go) _____ to the mall. My girlfriend knows this, so she usually chooses (4 go) _______ without me. |
| **Question 2** What kind of stores do you enjoy (5 go) _______ into? | Bookstores. I spend a lot of time (6 read) _____ book reviews so I always have a list of books I'd like (7 buy) _______. | I enjoy (8 look) _____ at electronic equipment but I can't afford (9 buy) _______ it. It's usually way too expensive. |
| **Question 3** Are there any kinds of stores you hate (10 go) _______ into? | I hate grocery stores. I usually forget (11 buy) _______ the things I went there for, so I avoid (12 go) _______ into them. Fortunately, I can do most of my food shopping online. | I refuse (13 go) _______ into shoe stores. I always decide (14 buy) _______ shoes online. It's easier and very straightforward. |
| **Question 4** Do you enjoy (15 buy) _______ clothes for yourself? | Not really. I only go into a clothing store when I need (16 buy) _______ a new shirt or something. For me, shopping is a necessity, not a pleasure. | I love (17 have) _______ new clothes, but I never manage (18 find) _______ time to go shopping. |

1.37 **Listen and check your answers. Do you know any men with similar attitudes?**

**Ask your partner the questions (1-4) from the interview.**

**2 Complete the following sentences with your own ideas.**

- **a** I enjoy ...
- **b** I don't mind ...
- **c** I can't stand ...
- **d** I avoid ...
- **e** I'd like ...
- **f** I need ...
- **g** I can't afford ...
- **h** I've decided ...

**Compare your sentences with your partner.**

## READING & VOCABULARY

**1 Look at the website and complete the descriptions with the words in the box.**

boots earrings pants shoes scarf
shirt skirt top jacket

runwayclothes.com

**runway** clothes

*get the look!*

Heidi is wearing a striped green linen (1) *top*, a blue leather (2)_______, colorful plastic (3)_______, and white and red leather (4)_______. All these items are on sale NOW - click here to get the look.

Ivan is wearing a black cotton (5) _______, a red silk (6) _______, a brown woolly (7)_______, black denim (8)_______, and black leather (9)_______. All these items could be yours TODAY - click here to get the look.

1.38 **Listen and check.**

**2 What do you think of the clothes in the pictures? Tell a partner.**

**3 Complete the table with words from the descriptions in Exercise 1 above.**

| Design/Color | Material | Clothes and accessories |
|---|---|---|
| *black* | *cotton* | *shirt* |
| | | |
| | | |

**4** 1.39 **Listen and repeat the items of clothing (a-d).**

a 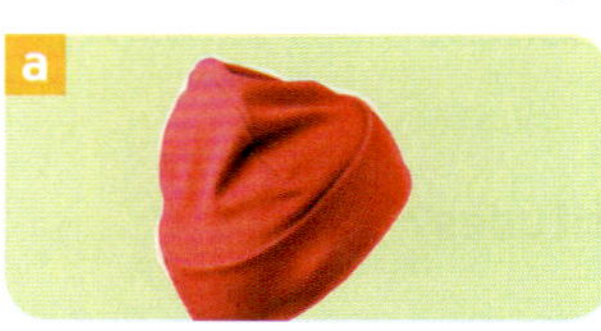

b 

c 

d 

**Add the words to the table in Exercise 3.**

**5 Complete the sentences below in as much detail as possible so that they are true for you. Compare your sentences with a partner.**

a I never wear ... b I often wear ... c Today, I'm wearing ...

*I never wear checked shirts. Today I'm wearing a blue cotton top.*

## READING

**1** **Read the article. Why is Edun different from other clothing companies?**

GROUP HOUSES BEHIND THE SCENES TALENTS INVESTORS

People are caring more and more these days about where their clothes come from. And this means companies like Edun are getting more attention.

Ali Hewson spent five weeks in Ethiopia, Africa, in 1985 during a major famine. After that, she created Edun with her husband, Bono, in 2005 because she wanted to bring more business into Africa.

Hewson thought that ethical fashion was a good place to start, but she felt that ethical clothing also needs to look good.

Edun had a rocky start, but in 2009 the luxury fashion company LVMH took a 49 per cent stake. These days the brand's dresses and leather skirts are selling on top fashion websites.

Ninety-five per cent of the collection is made in sub-Saharan Africa. There are two factories in Madagascar and one in Kenya. These factories are employing local people, mainly women, giving them good, stable jobs. And all the money is put back into the company – so there are no profits right now.

Bono doesn't attend fashion shows, but he's very involved with Edun. Hewson says that his priority is his "day job" – that is, singing in U2. "He's always encouraging us, and he gets what we're doing."

What's next? Hewson wants to expand the business because more trade with Africa will help improve people's lives. That is Hewson's mission.

**2** **Look at the words in the article and match to the meaning.**

- **a** famine (line 5)
- **b** ethical (line 9)
- **c** rocky (line 12)
- **d** collection (line 16)
- **e** stable (line 20)
- **f** mission (line 30)

1. being full of problems
2. goal; purpose
3. following the right moral behavior
4. in a good place which isn't going to change
5. a situation where people don't have enough food
6. a group of clothes created by a designer

**3** **Is the trend towards 'ethical clothing' happening in your country? Discuss these questions with your partner.**

- **a** Do people care where their clothes are made?
- **b** Do you think people want to pay more for 'ethical clothing'?

## GRAMMAR

**1** **Match the underlined verb forms (1–3) in these sentences with their uses (a–c).**

Today (1) I'm wearing a dress from Edun. (2) I usually wear cheap clothes, but these days (3) I'm buying more clothes from designers because they look so great.

- **a** Actions that happen **all the time, often, sometimes, never, etc.** (Simple present)
- **b** Actions that are **in progress at the moment of speaking.** (Present progressive)
- **c** Actions that are **in progress** around **the moment of speaking.** (Present progressive)

**Present tenses**

**Simple present**
I **work** in an office.
We **start** work at nine.

**Present progressive**
I'**m not working** now.
I'**m having** lunch.

My job is **getting** more difficult to do.

**2** **Write these sentences in the negative and match them with the uses (a–c) in Exercise 1.**

- **a** I'm sitting near the door.
  I'm not sitting near the door. = Use 'b'
- **b** My parents go to church.
- **c** I'm saving money for my next vacation.
- **d** My mother works in a bookstore.
- **e** I'm studying for an exam.
- **f** It's raining.
- **g** I'm learning to play the piano.
- **h** The cost of living is going up fast.

**Check (✓) the sentences – affirmative or negative – that are true. Compare with a partner.**

**3** Pairwork **Student A:** page ii **Student B:** page iv

**4** Grammar Extra 4, Part 2 page xi. Read the explanation and do the exercises.

## LANGUAGE FOR LIFE

**1 Russell wants to buy a gift for his girlfriend. Read the expressions. Put R if you think Russell says them. Put SC if you think the sales clerk says them.**

- **a** I'm just looking, thanks. [R]
- **b** I'll take it. [ ]
- **c** Can I help you? [ ]
- **d** What colors do you have? [ ]
- **e** How would you like to pay? [ ]
- **f** Can she exchange it if it doesn't fit? [ ]
- **g** What size is she? [ ]
- **h** Here's your receipt. [ ]
- **i** What sort of thing are you looking for? [ ]
- **j** By credit card. [ ]

1.40 **Listen, check, and repeat.**

**2 Put the expressions in the correct place in the conversation.**

SC: (1) *Can I help you?*
R: (2) ______________ Well, actually, I'm looking for something for my girlfriend.
SC: (3) ______________
R: I don't really know. A sweater?
SC: OK, and what color would you like?
R: (4) ______________
SC: We have any color you want, sir. Purple is very fashionable right now.
R: Purple's fine.
SC: OK. (5) ______________
R: Ah, well, she isn't very big, but she's not particularly small.
SC: So she's medium.
R: Yes, medium.
SC: Well, we have this nice purple sweater here ...
R: Good. (6) ______________
SC: Are you sure you don't want to see any more ...?
R: No, that's great. I'll take it. Thank you. How much is it?
SC: That's $70, sir. (7) ______________
R: Seventy?! (8) ______________ , please.
SC: Fine. If you could insert your code, please.
R: Here you go. Goodbye.
SC: Just a minute, sir. (9) ______________
R: Oh, yes, er ... (10) ______________
SC: Yes, but she needs to keep the receipt.

1.41 **Listen and check answers.**

**Practice the conversation with a partner.**

**3 Work with your partner. Write your own shopping conversation.**

- **a** Decide on the store and what the customer is buying.
- **b** Decide on the character/personality of the sales clerk and the customer.
- **c** Include at least six of these eight words.
- **d** Practice your conversation and perform it for the rest of the class.

by fit help
just pay receipt
size sort

### LIFE SKILLS: Planning
A Shopping Trip

**1** 1.42 **Listen to the conversation. Write down what Paul needs to get at the mall and where he has to go.**

Shopping list

| Item(s) | Store |
|---|---|
| | |
| | |
| | |
| | |

**2 Look at the shopping mall guide. Plan a route for Paul to pick up everything from his list using the words in the box. Compare with a partner.**

first next then after that finally

**CITYCENTER SHOPPING MALL GUIDE:**

| Level 1 | Level 2 | Level 3 | Level 4 |
|---|---|---|---|
| 101 Elite Sports | 201 The Phone Store | 301 Watertone Bookstore | 401 Fallow Travel |
| 102 Drinkin' Donuts | 202 Frankie's Stationery | 302 Don Read Drugstore | 402 Dry Cleaning 'R' Us |
| 103 Tammy's Gifts | 203 Olsen Jewelry | 303 Fallmark Cards | 403 The Flower Shop |
| 104 Stirruck's Coffee Shop | 204 All-in Groceries | 304 Mighty Games | |

MACMILLAN LIFE SKILLS

## Clothes and accessories

**1 Match the pictures with the descriptions. Then complete the descriptions.**

| | | |
|---|---|---|
| [7] a checked scarf | [ ] a pinstriped ______ | [ ] gold ______ |
| [ ] brown leather ______ | [ ] a silver ______ | [ ] striped ______ |
| [ ] a plain white cotton ______ | [ ] a patterned woolen ______ | [ ] plastic ______ |
| [ ] a blue denim ______ | [ ] a floral ______ | [ ] a light blue silk ______ |

**2 Work with a partner. Cover the words. Look at the pictures. Ask and answer questions.**

What's this?

It's a checked scarf.

What are these?

They're brown leather gloves.

## Focus on verbs used with clothes

**1 Match the verb phrases with their meanings.**

a get dressed
b get undressed
c get changed
d clothes fit you
e clothes look good on you
f try something on

1 take your clothes off
2 put something on to see if it fits/looks good on you
3 clothes are the right size for you
4 put your clothes on
5 clothes are the right color, shape, and style for you
6 take your clothes off and put different clothes on

**2 Underline the most appropriate verb phrase.**

a I always **get dressed** / **get undressed** before breakfast.
b I usually **try on** / **wear** formal clothes at work.
c When it's cold, I **put on** / **take off** my leather coat.
d I like **trying on** / **taking off** new clothes.
e Yellow and orange don't **look good on** / **fit** me.
f I **get dressed** / **get changed** when I get home from work.

**Check (✓) the sentences that are true for you. Compare with your partner.**

# 5 In shape

## READING

1 **Read the interview with a triathlete. Answer these questions.**

- Does she train all sports every day?
- Will she take part in events outside USA?

## FitterToday

Mindy, how did you become a triathlete?
I was good at swimming at high school, but I wasn't the best, so a coach said I should try out for the triathlon. And I crashed my bike in my first race! But I've improved ...

How often do you train for the triathlon?
Every single day. You can't stop, really. I try to run, swim, and ride every morning. But each day I focus on one area more than the others.

How often do you compete in a triathlon?
Well, at the moment I do about five or six events over the summer here in the United States. But next year I'll join the World Triathlon Series.

How many miles do you run?
I usually run about 10 kilometers in the morning, on a 'running day'.

How far do you ride on a 'bike day'?
I try to ride the triathlon distance, which is 40 kilometers.

How long does it take to ride 40km?
Some days, it takes about an hour and fifteen minutes. It really depends on the day!

How many events are there in the World Series?
The series is 10 events from March to September. It's a long season, but I'm ready for it.

2 **Complete the statements with the correct number.**

a Triathletes need to train for __three__ sports.
b Mindy runs ________ kilometers on a running day.
c The bike ride in a triathlon is ________ kilometers.
d Some days, it takes Mindy ________ minutes to complete the cycle distance.
e Mindy hopes to compete in ________ events next year.

3 **What extreme sport would you like to try? Discuss with a partner.**

- **Grammar:** Comparatives and superlatives. Phrasal verbs.
- **Vocabulary:** *How* + adjective/adverb. Sports. Numbers.
- **Language for Life:** Giving instructions

## VOCABULARY

1 **Look at the table. How long does it take you to do each activity?**
Guess the time it takes your partner to do the same things.
Ask your partner questions to check your ideas.

| **Activity :** How long does it take you to ... | | | |
|---|---|---|---|
| 1 get up in the morning? | | 5 read a novel? | |
| 2 buy gifts for people you love? | | 6 get ready to go out for the evening? | |
| 3 choose from a menu in a restaurant? | | 7 get to sleep at night? | |
| 4 decide whether you like someone? | | | |

**Guess the time it takes for your partner to do the same things.**
**Ask your partner questions to check your ideas.**

How long does it take you to get up in the morning?

About twenty minutes.

2 **Complete more questions with *How* + adjective/adverb. Use the words in the box.**

far fast long many much often

a How _often_ do you travel by train?
b How ________ does it take you to get to work or school?
c How ________ cousins do you have?
d How ________ cash do you have with you right now?
e How ________ is it from your house to the nearest beach?
f How ________ does your car go?

**Ask your partner the questions.**

## SPEAKING: ANECDOTE

1 1.43 **Listen to Tina talking about her experiences of doing sports at school.**
**Are the answers here right (✓) or wrong (✖)?**

a How many hours of sports did you do each week at school?
**Three hours a week.** ✖
b What different sports did you do during the school year?
**Swimming, tennis, and lacrosse.**
c Which sports did you like/hate the most?
**I hated lacrosse.**
d What kind of sports facilities did your school have?
**A gym and a basketball court.**
e Did you ever play for a school team?
**Yes, I played for the school lacrosse team.**

2 **You're going to tell your partner about your experiences of doing sports at school.**
- Ask yourself the questions in Exercise 1.
- Think about *what* to say and *how* to say it.
- Tell your partner about your experiences of doing sports at school.

## LISTENING

1 **Work with a partner. Try to match each of these famous sports stars with their date of birth.**

### Date of birth:

- [*e*] 04/19/1987
- [ ] 02/05/1985
- [ ] 05/04/1989
- [ ] 03/14/1997
- [ ] 03/14/1988
- [ ] 02/05/1992

a Ronaldo

b Rory McIlroy

c Simone Biles

d Stephen Curry

e Maria Sharapova

f Neymar

1.44 **Listen and check your answers.**

2 1.45 **Listen to a discussion between a marketing director and an advertising executive. Which sports star do they choose to advertise a new energy drink?**

**Listen again and complete these sentences.**

a *Sharapova* is more famous than *McIlroy*.
b ________ is more popular than ________.
c ________ is not as old as ________.
d ________ much more popular than ________.
e ________ is much younger than ________.

3 **Work with a partner. List the most famous sports stars in your country. Complete the sentences in Exercise 2 with names from your list. Choose one star from your list to advertise a car. Compare with other students in the class.**

## GRAMMAR & VOCABULARY

1 **Test your general knowledge! Use the adjective in parentheses with *a little bit / much / not as … as* to make true comparisons.**

a London (wet) ________ Rome. *London is not as wet as Rome.*
b Hawaii (big) ________ Cuba.
c The Mall of America (small) ________ the Dubai Mall.
d Heathrow Airport in London (busy) ________ Los Angeles International Airport.
e Big Ben (tall) ________ the Statue of Liberty.

1.46 **Listen and check your answers.**

**Comparatives**

He's **a little bit older**
He's **older** **than** her.
He's **much older**

She's **not as old as** him.

2 **Combine the noun phrases with the adjectives to make comparative statements that you agree with.**

Chilean nuts flying German cars living in a city men Mexican food shopping online women

cheap complex convenient exciting expensive funny interesting noisy reliable safe sensitive sophisticated

**Compare your statements with a partner. Do you agree or disagree?**

3 **Grammar Extra 5, Part 1** page xiii. Read the explanation and do the exercises.

## PRONUNCIATION

1 **Complete the following expressions with the appropriate word.**

a It's as light as a *feather*.
b He's as free as a ______.
c They're as good as ______.
d She's as pretty as a ______.
e It's as solid as a ______.
f It's as old as the ______.

2 1.47 **Listen, check, and repeat. Practice the red schwa (/ə/) sounds.**
**Can you think of people or things you could describe in this way? Do you have similar expressions in your language?**

## GRAMMAR

1 **Write out the superlative forms for the following groups of adjectives.**

| Adjectives | Superlative forms |
|---|---|
| a old / rich / exciting / great | *the oldest / the richest / the ...* |
| b valuable / big / hot / thin | |
| c funny / interesting / sexy / happy | |
| d bad / far / good / talented | |

**In each group, underline the superlative adjective which is formed in a different way.**

**Superlatives**

**Short adjectives**
the rich**est**,
the bigg**est**,
the funni**est**

**Irregular forms**
the **best**, the **worst**,
the **furthest**

**Long adjectives**
the **most** interesting,
the **most** modern

2 **Complete the questions with different superlative adjectives. Use the adjectives in Exercise 1 or your own ideas.**

a Who is ______ sports person in the world?
b What is ______ music group of all time?
c What is ______ place you've ever visited?
d Who is ______ person you know?
e What is ______ possession you have?

**Ask a partner your questions.**

## VOCABULARY

1 1.48 **Listen and repeat the numbers in the box.**

| ¾ 0.25 0.33 1½ ⅛ ¼ 1.5 0.125 ⅓ 0.75 |
|---|

**Make pairs of numbers with the same value. Practice saying the numbers.**
*¾ is the same as 0.75.*

2 1.49 **Listen and repeat the numbers in column A. Write each number in full.**

| | A | B |
|---|---|---|
| *two hundred and sixty-three kilometers an hour* | a 263 km/h | 1 Cristiano Ronaldo's earnings |
| | b 42.195 km | 2 The biggest soccer score |
| | c $70,600,000 | 3 The fastest tennis serve |
| | d 31-0 | 4 The official distance for a marathon |

**Match the numbers in column A with the facts in column B.**

3 **Pairwork Student A:** page ii **Student B:** page iv

## READING

1 Look at the picture and read the posts about how people relax. Who would you like to be?

Facebook | Instagram | Youtube

http:// instagram.com

Instagram

lizziebeach **Follow**

**lizziebeach** This is how I relax: I turn off the phone, give up social media, hang up my hammock and have a nap in the afternoon. I just hear the sound of the waves and feel the breeze on my face. #howdoyouchill

**samsuit** This is good! I would like to take off my shoes, throw away my diary and go to the beach. #howdoyouchill

**donnyboy** Yes, it's time to relax. I'm not going to turn on the computer this morning. I'm going to just sit on the balcony with my cup of coffee and watch people on the street. #howdoyouchill

**paula22** You have inspired me! I'm going to put on my headphones and just go and walk in the park. Summertime is here! #howdoyouchill

**frannie9** I can't turn off my phone, and I can't give up social media – it's my job! But I will soon have my vacation. A full month to relax. #howdoyouchill

57 likes

1 DAY AGO

Add a comment...

2 **Discuss the questions with a partner.**

a What do you do to relax?

b What stops you from relaxing?

## VOCABULARY

1 **Complete the sentences using the phrasal verbs in the box.**

| give up | hang up | put on | ~~take off~~ | throw away | turn off | turn on |
|---|---|---|---|---|---|---|

a I always <u>take off</u> my shoes before I go into my house.

b If I want to relax, I __________ all the lights and sit in silence.

c When I want to look my best, I __________ a suit.

d I could never __________ coffee – it's the only thing that keeps me awake.

e The first thing I do when I get to the office is __________ my computer.

f I never __________ plastic bags because they're so useful.

g I never do any ironing. I just __________ my clothes very carefully when they are wet.

2 **Are any of the sentences true for you? Discuss with your partner.**

## GRAMMAR

1 **Work with a partner. Look at the three phrasal verbs used in these sentences (*take off*, *run after*, and *sit down*) and answer the questions.**

| subject | verb | object | particle | | subject | verb | particle | object |
|---|---|---|---|---|---|---|---|---|
| I | took | my shoes | off | and | I | ran | after | the bus. |

But it didn't stop.

| | subject | verb | particle | |
|---|---|---|---|---|
| So | I | sat | down | and cried. I hate bus drivers. |

**Phrasal verbs**

**Intransitive**
She **sat down**.

**Transitive (separable)**
He **took off** his shoes.
He **took** his shoes **off**.
He **took** them **off**.

**Transitive (not separable)**
They **ran after** the bus.
They **ran after** it.

a Which phrasal verb does not take an object? (INTRANSITIVE)
b Which phrasal verb can have the object between the verb and the particle? (TRANSITIVE - SEPARABLE)
c Which phrasal verb always has the object after the particle? (TRANSITIVE - NOT SEPARABLE)

2 **When the object is a pronoun such as *it*, *them*, *her*, where do you always put it when the phrasal verb is: a) separable? b) inseparable?**

3 **Put the words in the correct order to make answers to the questions. Look the phrasal verbs up in a dictionary if you are not sure.**

a What should I do with this banana skin? (away / throw / it) Throw it away.
b What should I do with this mess? (it / up / clear)
c What should I do with my pants? (hang / up / them)
d What should I do about this problem? (it / deal / with)
e What should I do with this application form? (fill / in / it)
f What should I do about my party? Nobody can come. (it / call / off)

4 **Grammar Extra 5, Part 2 page xiii. Read the explanation and do the exercises.**

## LISTENING & SPEAKING

1 **You are going to listen to a radio show about laughter clubs. Do you think the statements (a-e) are true or false?**

a Young children laugh much more than adults.
b Laughter clubs started in the USA.
c Laughter releases happy chemicals called endorphins.
d Laughing is good for the heart.
e In laughter clubs, people laugh at funny stories.

1.50 **Listen and check your answers.**

2 **Face your partner. Take turns trying to make each other laugh.**

3 **Work with your partner. Discuss the following questions.**

a What kind of thing makes you laugh?
b How do you feel after a good laugh?
c When was the last time you laughed so much you couldn't stop?

## LANGUAGE FOR LIFE

**1** 1.51 **Listen to the three conversations (a-c). Which sports are these people learning?**

**a** Selma's learning to _______________.

**b** Jimmy's learning to play _______________.

**c** Rebecca's learning to play _______________.

**2 Match each person in Exercise 1 with a set of instructions *1*, *2*, or *3*.**

**1** Throw the ball in the air.
Don't look at me.
Look at the ball.
Pick up your racket.
Try again.

**2** Stand up on the board.
Hold on.
Don't let go.
Be careful.
Don't go too fast.

**3** Kick the ball.
Don't throw the ball.
Don't pick it up.
Don't touch the ball with your hand.
Use your foot.

**3 Complete the first conversation in Exercise 1 by replacing the highlighted phrases (1-6) with the useful phrases in the box.**

Be careful! Be patient. Come back! ~~Don't be mean.~~ Don't worry. Try again.

**Paul:** OK, are you ready?
**Selma:** Yes.
**Paul:** Stand up on the board.
**Selma:** OK. Ohhhh!
**Paul:** Ha, ha, ha!
**Selma:** (**1**) Be nice. *Don't be mean.*
**Paul:** Oh, sorry. OK. (**2**) Don't give up. Good! Great. Hold on. Don't let go.
**Selma:** Ohhhh! It's too difficult. I can't do it.
**Paul:** Nonsense! Of course you can do it. (**3**) Don't be impatient. Come on, try again.
**Selma:** I look silly.
**Paul:** (**4**) Relax. Everyone looks silly the first time. Now, stand up on the board. That's it. (**5**) Take care! Good. Now, don't go too fast, Selma. Selma! (**6**) Don't go too far!
**Selma:** Wheeee!

**Listen to the conversation again and check. Practice the conversation with a partner.**

### LIFE SKILLS: Time Management
An Exercise Routine

**1 Match the phrases (a-f) with the pictures (1-6).**

a a push up
b a squat
c a pull up
d a plank
e jog in place
f a lunge

1.52 **Listen, check, and repeat.**

**2** 1.53 **Listen to the podcast. What exercises does it include?**

**3 Create your own timed workout routine. Compare with a partner.**

1

2

3

4

5

6

MACMILLAN LIFE SKILLS

# 5 Vocabulary Extra

## Clothes and accessories

1 **Complete the table. Use the pictures of equipment to help you.**

| Sports | Person | Place | Equipment |
|---|---|---|---|
| track | a runner | an athletics track | shorts, a running top, (**1**) running shoes |
| skiing | a skier | a ski resort | skis, ski boots, ski poles, (**2**) ___________ |
| soccer | a soccer player | a soccer field | a soccer ball, shorts, a soccer shirt, (**3**) ___________ |
| golf | a golfer | a golf course | golf balls, (**4**) ___________ |
| swimming | a swimmer | a swimming pool | a swimsuit, (**5**) ___________ (**6**) ___________ |
| tennis | a tennis player | a tennis court | tennis balls, (**7**) ___________, (**8**) ___________ |

2 **Add more words or sports to the table in Exercise 1. Use your dictionary.**

## Focus on verbs used with sports

1 **Underline the most appropriate alternative in each of these sentences.**

a I **do** / **play** / **practice** some exercise two or three times a week. It keeps me in shape.
b I've never **been** / **played** / **practiced** windsurfing. I can't swim.
c I'd like to **play** / **go** / **practice** snowboarding. I love the mountains.
d The last time I **did** / **went** / **practiced** some sports was on vacation.
e I **did** / **played** / **practiced** a lot of baseball when I was a child. Now I just watch it on TV.
f I'm not very good at tennis because I don't have time to **do** / **go** / **practice**.

**How many of the sentences are true for you? Compare with a partner.**

2 **Complete the verb phrases with *do*, *go*, or *play*. Use your dictionary and add more sports to each list.**

| a ___________ | b ___________ | c ___________ |
|---|---|---|
| cycling | athletics | basketball |
| fishing | judo | golf |
| swimming | | tennis |
| windsurfing | | volleyball |

# 6 Job

## LISTENING

**1** 1.54 **Listen to four people giving answers to the same question. What was the question?**

a

Mark, a CEO

b
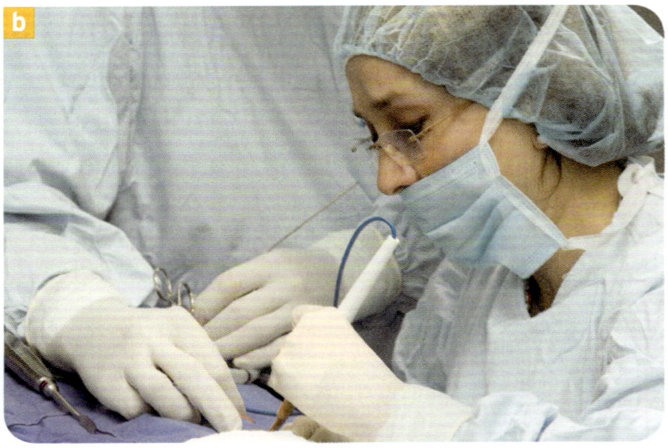
Karen, a surgeon

c

Frank, a teacher

d

Mia, a model

**2 Listen again and check (✓) the jobs that each person mentions.**

| | | | | | |
|---|---|---|---|---|---|
| Mark: | a soldier ☑ | an engineer ☐ | a DJ ☐ | a CEO ☐ | |
| Karen: | a surgeon ☐ | a ballet dancer ☐ | a doctor ☐ | a tour guide ☐ | a butcher ☐ |
| Frank: | a farmer ☐ | a vet ☐ | a pilot ☐ | a snowboarder ☐ | a teacher ☐ |
| Mia: | an archaeologist ☐ | an au pair ☐ | a model ☐ | a telemarketer ☐ | |

**What did you want to be when you were a child?**

## SPEAKING

**1 Work as a class. Write the names of all the jobs that you, your parents, and your grandparents have had.**

**2 Work in small groups. Look at all the jobs you wrote down in Exercise 1 and discuss these questions.**

a In which job can you earn the most money?
b In which job do you get the most vacation days?
c Which job do you study the longest for?
d In which job do you need the most training?
e Which job is the most stressful?
f Which job is the most useful to society?

- **Grammar:** Permission and obligation (*can/ have to*). Present perfect and simple past.
- **Vocabulary:** Jobs. Collocations (work). *should*. Office equipment.
- **Language for Life:** Presenting yourself

## READING

1 **You are going to read an article about a dream job. What do you think is the best job in the world? Discuss with a partner.**

2 **Read the article. Answer the questions.**

a What is the job?
b What are the qualifications?
c How do you apply?

**BCCB News**

home news sport entertainment **lifestyle**

14 January share

### *Best Job In The World?*

***Beth Rigby***

Vacations are an escape from all the screens in your life, but you'll probably post photos and videos about your trip on social media, right? So why not get paid for it?

A vacation company, Luxury Vacation Homes, is looking for applicants for a job where you can get paid to travel all over the world for three months. Your task? Well, you have to stay in 12 luxury vacation homes and share your experiences on social media. Not too tough, right? Although it's only a temporary job, the company pays $10,000 a month and covers all travel expenses!

The company describes the position as "the best job on the planet." And I can see why. You can take your friends with you (but they can't come for free) and you can choose your own itinerary.

To apply for the job, make a one-minute video explaining exactly why you're the best candidate for the best job on the planet. You don't have to make a professional video, but you have to send it to Luxury Vacation Homes before March 30.

The bottom line: now might be a good time to drop everything and work on your application video. Get ready for an extended vacation. Best of luck.

## GRAMMAR

1 **Match the underlined part of each sentence from the article (a-d) with the correct meaning (1-4).**

a You can take your friends.
b They can't come for free.
c You have to stay in vacation homes.
d You don't have to make a professional video.

1 It's necessary for me to ...
2 It isn't OK for them to ...
3 It isn't necessary for me to ...
4 It's OK for me to ...

2 **Match the beginnings and ends of these sentences so that they make sense.**

a A snowboarder
b A club DJ
c A flight attendant
d A tour guide
e A model
f A cook

1 can get up late.
2 has to have very clean hands.
3 has to wear a crash helmet.
4 can't eat fattening food.
5 has to know a lot of history.
6 doesn't have to pay for flights.

**Think about your work or school. Which can you do and what do you have to do?**

3 Grammar Extra 6, Part 1 page xv. **Read the explanation and do the exercises.**

**can / can't**
**have to / don't have to**

*can* = It's permitted.
*can't* = It isn't permitted.

You **can** vote at 18, but you **can't** fly a plane until you are 21.

*have to* = It's necessary.
*don't have to* = It isn't necessary.

You **have to** wear a helmet on a motorcycle, but you **don't have to** wear one on a bicycle.

## READING

**1 Work with a partner. Discuss the bad experiences you could have in these jobs.**

an au pair | a waiter/waitress | a sales clerk | a lifeguard | a factory worker

**2 Read the tweets. Which do you think is the worst first job?**

**New Jobs** @newjobfair 4h

Follow

As our job fair begins today, we want to hear about your first job using the hashtag **#myfirstjob**

**Dan Ley** @danielley6 3h
I was a part-time sales clerk at my local convenience store. One day, I took my break and just never went back … after that, I had to go three miles to another store to do my shopping! #myfirstjob

**Saskia Phillips** @theatersaskia 3h
I hated my first job. I was an au pair and had to look after 4 terrible kids. I had one day off a week, but I was so exhausted that I slept all day. I stayed in the job for six months before I moved to New York to become an actor. #myfirstjob

**Sam Olive** @ samanthaolive3 2h
I HAVE to get a job somewhere else. My first (and current job) is in a factory – it's so hot and boring. And you have to ask for permission to have breaks. Save me! #myfirstjob

**Pete Kirtley** @ peterkirtley 52m
My first job was as a waiter. It was really hard work, and without tips it was very difficult to make a living. I now own my restaurant and make sure my team keep all their tips! #myfirstjob

**Tim Thomas** @ timmyt 14m
My first job was perfect – I was the lifeguard at the local country club pool. The pool was often empty, so I just sat in the sun listening to music. Easy money! #myfirstjob

**3 Answer the questions. Read again and check your answers.**

a Who's working in a factory?
b Who's now an actor?
c Who's worked as a waiter?
d Who's had a perfect first job?
e Who took a break and never came back?
f Who's taken care of children?

## VOCABULARY

**1 Add another collocation to each of the sets below using words and phrases from the tweets above.**

a to have **some time** / **two weeks** / ___a day off___ (Saskia)
b to **find** / **lose** / __________ a job (Sam)
c to make **a decision** / **money** / __________ (Pete)
d a **well-paid** / **full-time** / __________ job (Dan)
e to take a **nap** / **rest** / __________ (Dan)
f to ask for **advice** / **a pay-raise** / __________ to have breaks (Sam)

**2 Use any collocations from Exercise 1 to write six sentences about yourself.**

*The last time I had some time off was at Thanksgiving.*
*I'd like to find a part-time job.*

## GRAMMAR

**1 Look at these two sentences and answer the questions below.**

1 *Yes, I had various jobs when I was a student.*
2 *So I've had lots of part-time jobs over the years.*

a Which sentence refers to a completed action in "finished" time? What tense is used?
b Which sentence refers to a completed action in time "up to now"? What tense is used?

**Present perfect**

| | |
|---|---|
| I**'ve** | |
| You**'ve** | **worked** |
| He/She/**It's** | **seen** |
| We**'ve** | **been** |
| They**'ve** | |

I**'ve** = I **have**
He**'s** = He **has**

**Have** you ever **worked** in a bar?
Yes, I **have**.
No, I **haven't**.
(*ever* = at any time "up to now")

**2 Complete the table with the time expressions in the box.**

a few minutes ago in 2015 in the last two weeks
last week never over the years recently
this week today when I was a student years ago

| "Finished" time | Time "up to now" |
|---|---|
| *a few minutes ago* | *in the last two weeks* |
| | |
| | |
| | |
| | |

**3 Complete the sentences with time expressions from Exercise 2, or some of your own. Write true sentences using the appropriate tense for the verb in parentheses.**

a I (buy) ________ a new phone ...
*I bought a new phone last week.*
b I (not go) ________ to the beach ...
c I (meet) ________ some interesting people ...
d I (spend) ________ a lot of money ...
e I (not see) ________ any good movies ...
f I (do) ________ a lot of silly things ...
g I (read) ________ *Pride and Prejudice* ...
h I (lose) ________ my keys ...

**4** Pairwork **Student A:** page ii **Student B:** page iv

**5** Grammar Extra 6, Part 2 **page xv. Read the explanation and do the exercises.**

## PRONUNCIATION

**1 Complete the table with the past participles of these irregular verbs. Underline the past participle in each group with a different vowel sound.**

| Infinitive | Past participle |
|---|---|
| a say read feed see | *said read fed* *<u>seen</u>* |
| b know buy fly grow | |
| c ring sing bring hang | |
| d drink teach think fight | |

1.55 **Listen, check, and repeat.**

## SPEAKING

**1 Work with a partner. Make questions from the following prompts.**

a best or worst / party / ever go to
*What's the best party you've ever been to?*
b best or worst / vacation / ever go on
c best or worst / meal / ever eat
d best or worst / joke / ever hear
e best or worst / car / ever go in
f best or worst / T-shirt / ever wear
g best or worst / bed / ever sleep in

**2 Choose three questions from Exercise 1 and ask your partner. Find out as much as you can.**

What's the best vacation you've ever been on?

When I went to Australia.

When did you go?

## LISTENING

**1 Look at the picture of Mr. McClusky. You are going to listen to a radio interview with him. Work with a partner and discuss possible answers to these questions.**

a What kind of company does Mr. McClusky work for?
b When did he start working for the company?
c How old is he now?

**2 1.56 Listen and check your ideas.**

**3 Listen again and decide if these statements are true or false. Correct the false statements to make them true.**

a Mr. McClusky never forces anybody to retire. True.
b The oldest employee at McClusky's is 97. False. He's 87.
c McClusky's pays a decent salary.
d Employees get five weeks of paid vacation.
e All the staff members are over the retirement age.
f Mr. McClusky's secretary Barbara had to resign because she wanted to get married.
g Mr. McClusky's brother is going to run the business from next year.

## VOCABULARY

**1 Use the appropriate underlined words and expressions in Exercise 3 above to complete these statements.**

a Everybody should get six weeks of paid vacation a year.
b Firefighters, teachers, and police officers don't get a _______. They should get more money.
c The official _______ should be the same for men and women.
d If you don't want _______, you should be able to continue working.
e CEOs who _______ large corporations shouldn't earn such large salaries.
f Politicians who tell lies should _____.

**2 Check (✓) the ending that best describes the meaning of *should* in the statements in Exercise 1.**

| You use *should* when you think something is ... | | |
|---|---|---|
| | a funny idea. | ☐ |
| | a good idea. | ☐ |
| | a strange idea. | ☐ |

**3 Work in small groups. Do you agree or disagree with the statements in Exercise 1?**

## WRITING

**1** **Read this email applying for a job at McClusky's Department Store. Use the words and expressions in the box to improve the parts of the letter that are highlighted.**

| | | |
|---|---|---|
| a new challenge | attached | look forward to hearing |
| reached retirement age | Sir or Madam: | would like to apply for |

Dear (1) McClusky: Sir or Madam:

I saw your advertisement for a position as sales clerk in your homeware department and I (2) want the job.

I am an experienced sales clerk and I have worked in many different departments. Please see my resume, (3) in a different document, for more details.

I started working in sales when I was twenty-one, forty-five years ago. I left my last job six years ago when I (4) got too old, but I get terribly bored at home. I feel I am ready for (5) new things now.

I would be available for an interview at any time, even at short notice.

I (6) can't wait to hear from you.

Sincerely,

Michele Stern

Michele Stern (Ms.)

**2** **Write your own email applying for your dream job.**

## SPEAKING: ANECDOTE

**1** 1.57 **Listen to Kim talking about her friend's job. Underline the answers she gives.**

- **a** What's his or her name? Her name's Hannah / Ann.
- **b** What does she do? She's a **train driver / personal trainer.**
- **c** Who does she work for? **She works for a local sports center / She's self-employed.**
- **d** What time does she start work? At **7:00 / 8:30 a.m.**
- **e** How much does she earn? She gets **$35 / $25** an hour.
- **f** What does she love about her job? **She helps people get in shape / She travels a lot.**
- **g** Would you like to have your friend's job? Why? **Yes, because she doesn't have to work in an office / No, because she has to get up early.**

**2** **You're going to tell your partner about somebody you know who has a good job.**

- Ask yourself the questions in Exercise 1.
- Think about *what* to say and *how* to say it.
- Tell your partner about the person's job.

## LANGUAGE FOR LIFE

**1** 1.58 **Listen to four people presenting themselves to the *Volunteer Program*. Underline the correct information.**

**Layla:** I work for a big company and we produce **sports clothing / audio equipment / bicycles.**
I'm responsible for sales and **promotion / quality control / advertising.**

**Mike:** Right now, I'm **working for my father / unemployed / training to be an engineer.**
I'm looking for a job in **publishing / the theater / tourism.**

**Jack:** I work as a bodyguard and I'm based **in the south / at head office / in Detroit.**
My job involves **a lot of foreign travel / import and export / sitting at my desk all day.**

**Elise:** I run **the photography department / the accounts department / my own company.**
I'm in charge of **a department / marketing / taking pictures.**

**2** **Three people arrive late for the group. Read the notes and use words from Exercise 1 to complete their presentations.**

**Sarah**
- Receptionist, Cutters Salon
- Responsible for appointments and accounts

Hi, I'm Sarah. I work (1) _as_ a receptionist (2) _____ Cutters Salon. I'm in (3) _____ of appointments and accounts.

**Charles**
- Tour Guide, City Tours
- Takes tourists around Boston
- Wants to be a hotel manager

I'm Charles. I'm a tour guide and I work (4) _____ City Tours. My job (5) _____ taking tourists around Boston. Right now, I'm (6) _____ for a job (7) _____ hotel management.

**Andrew**
- CEO of Luxe Autos
- Sells expensive cars
- In Salt Lake City

My name's Andrew. I (8) _____ a company called Luxe Autos. We (9) _____ expensive cars. We're (10) _____ in Salt Lake City.

1.59 **Listen and check your answers.**

**3** **Write a short presentation of yourself. Use true information or invent information based on your ideal job. Use three or more useful phrases from Exercise 1.**

### LIFE SKILLS: Negotiating
Who's Doing It?

**1** 1.60 **Listen to Beatrice and Nathan discuss sharing tasks. Write B if Beatrice agrees to do the task. Write N if Nathan agrees to do the task.**

| Tasks: | | | | |
|---|---|---|---|---|
| | Get stationery items | ☐ | Make the coffee | ☐ |
| | Write the report | ☐ | Do the filing | ☐ |
| | Print out the report | ☐ | Set up the conference room | ☐ |

**2** **What tasks do you have to do at work or school that you don't like to do? Write five tasks.**

| Tasks: | | |
|---|---|---|
| | 1 _______ | 4 _______ |
| | 2 _______ | 5 _______ |
| | 3 _______ | |

**3** **Work with a partner. Try to get your partner to help you with some of your tasks.**

MACMILLAN LIFE SKILLS

# 6 Vocabulary Extra

## Office equipment

**1 Match the pictures with the words.**

| | | | | | | | |
|---|---|---|---|---|---|---|---|
| a briefcase | 15 | a folder | ____ | a note pad | ____ | a printer | ____ |
| a calculator | ____ | a hole punch | ____ | paper clips | ____ | a screen | ____ |
| a desk lamp | ____ | a keyboard | ____ | a photocopier | ____ | a stapler | ____ |
| a filing cabinet | ____ | a mouse | ____ | Post-its | ____ | a trash can | ____ |

**2 Work with a partner. Cover the words and look at the pictures. Ask and answer questions.**

What's number 1?

A printer.

What's number 2?

Paper clips.

## Focus on *work* and *job*

**1 Work with a partner. Complete the following questions with *job* or *work* and then ask each other the questions.**

a Have you ever had a part-time ____?

b Would you like to ____ abroad?

c Do you know anybody who has a dangerous ____?

**2 Make more questions by replacing the highlighted words in Exercise 1 with appropriate alternatives from the box.**

| | | | | | |
|---|---|---|---|---|---|
| applied for | badly paid | boring | from home | in marketing | looked for |
| lost | outdoors | resigned from | stressful | well-paid | |

**Ask and answer six more questions with your partner.**

# Review B

## GRAMMAR

Grammar Extra **pages xi–xvi.**

**1 Put the adverbs of frequency in the correct position.**

a We get up at 7:00 a.m. (always)
*We always get up at 7:00 a.m.*
b You get to class on time! (never)
c We eat meat. (occasionally)
d They are at home on Sunday evenings. (often)
e Cecilia goes out in the evening. (hardly ever)

**Rewrite each sentence to make it true for you.**

a *I never get up at 7:00 a.m.*

**2 Complete the sentences with the comparative or superlative form of the adjectives in the box.**

| cheap | expensive | good-looking | healthy | noisy | sensitive |
|---|---|---|---|---|---|

a Jim runs and swims. He's the *healthiest* man I know.
b Jo is crying again. She's much more ______ than I thought.
c This old car only costs $2,000! It's not as ______ as that new one.
d Matt is so handsome – he's the ______ man in the class!
e I have $20. Which is the ______ suit in the shop?
f Be quiet, Max! ... Why are you so much ______ than Felipe?

**3 Complete the text with the simple present or present progressive form of the verbs.**

I (1 love) *love* shopping and I especially (2 like) ______ shopping for clothes! So I (3 have) ______ a lot of clothes. My eldest sister (4 not understand) ______. She (5 have) ______ four pairs of pants, two skirts, two pairs of shoes, and ten T-shirts. Of course I never (6 wear) ______ most of my clothes. So right now I (7 try) ______ to wear my old clothes and I (8 not buy) ______ any more new clothes. I (9 save) ______ money, but I (10 look) ______ terrible!

**4 Underline the correct words.**

OK, everybody. Mr. Smith says the exam starts at 10:00, but we all (1) **have to** / **can't** arrive ten minutes before then. He says we (2) **have to** / **don't have to** register at the desk before the exam. We (3) **can** / **have to** take money, cell phones, pens, and pencils into the exam room with us, but we (4) **can** / **can't** take any large bags. Oh, and we (5) **have to** / **can't** turn off our cell phones.

**5 Complete the conversation with the simple past or present perfect forms of the verbs.**

**A:** Hi. I'm interested in the sales clerk job.
**B:** (1 you work) *Have you worked* in a store before?
**A:** No, but I (2 do) ______ lots of shopping!
**B:** Oh. (3 you have) ______ any other jobs?
**A:** Yes, I (4 be) ______ a waitress, and last year I (5 work) ______ as an au pair in Seattle. I (6 go) ______ to Seattle after I (7 finish) ______ school. Wonderful shopping!

## VOCABULARY

**1 Put the words in the correct group.**

a a box of *chocolates, tissues*
b a bunch of ...
c a can of ...
d a bottle of ...

**2 Underline the word that doesn't belong in each group.**

a necklace cotton leather silk
b patterned plain boots striped
c earrings gloves shirt woolen
d checked jacket shoes skirt

**3 Match the beginnings and endings to make questions.**

a How long
b How far
c How many
d How often
e How much
f How well

1 do you watch movies in English?
2 do you know your teacher?
3 money did you spend today?
4 pairs of gloves do you have?
5 is it from your house to the store?
6 does it take you to get home in the evening?

**Ask and answer the questions with a partner.**

**4 Underline the best collocation to complete the sentences.**

a I don't like working every day. I want a **full-time** / **part-time** job.
b I don't earn much. I need to ask for **advice** / **a pay-raise**.
c Leave your job or stay - you should make a **living** / **decision**!
d I work all the time. I need some **day** / **time** off.
e Juan isn't working right now. He **found** / **lost** his job last week.

## PRONUNCIATION

**1 Look at some words from Units 4-6. Say the words and add them to the table.**

advice afford au pair avoid company doctor flowers horrible interested leather quality racket receive sandals talented valuable

| | | | |
|---|---|---|---|
| A ●• *doctor* | | | |
| B •● *advice* | | | |
| C ●•• *horrible* | | | |
| | | | |

**2 Underline the stressed syllable in each word.**

1.61 **Listen, check, and repeat.**

## READING & LISTENING

**1 Read the posts and answer the questions.**

a How are Johnny and Clara related?
b How does Clara feel about Johnny?

**Johnny D.**
2h ago

As it's Clara's party this evening, (her thirty-fifth? Unbelievable!), I just wanted to say a few words about our lovely Clara …

Clara and I are very different. She's a lot older (sorry!), much more sensible, and more ambitious. I'm quite relaxed about my life.

That's why Clara is the very successful owner and CEO of a cosmetic company … and I'm still studying for a PhD at college! It's also why Clara is a lot healthier than me. She gets up at 5:00 a.m. to go for one of her famous runs. She loves to stay in shape, and she looks great. I never get up before 9:00 a.m. And exercise for me is walking the 100 meters to the bus stop. Clara is also a lot smarter than me. I'm in jeans every day, she's in sharp skirts or designer dresses. And those heels!

But the best thing about Clara is how kind and generous she is. I'm glad she's part of our family and that we've become very close. So, Clara, have a wonderful birthday. Here's to you!

Like Comment Share

Write a comment...

**Clara Richardson**
1h ago

Thank you (I think!) to Johnny for his post. Now, it's my turn!

Yes, I am 35 today. So, I'm older than Johnny by, er, a few years – but luckily he makes me feel young! He may be a bit lazy (how long to finish a degree?!) but it's been great getting to know him over the last few years.

We are very different. He doesn't like any exercise – I get very grumpy if I haven't run 5km each morning, but he spends most of his weekend on his couch. He always wears old T-shirts, jeans, and sneakers – I just hope he sometimes washes them. I like to wear nice dresses, shoes, and jewelry. I have a company to run, so I have to make a good impression!

But Johnny is a great listener, and he always calms me down when I'm getting angry about something. Finally, I'm so glad that our parents got married so I can say that Johnny is my stepbrother. Actually forget the 'step' – I'm proud to have Johnny as my brother.

Like Comment Share

Write a comment...

**2 Read the posts again. Are these statements true or false?**

a Johnny is older than Clara. *False*
b Johnny runs his own company.
c Johnny and Clara both like to exercise in the morning.
d Johnny and Clara both like wearing jeans and T-shirts.
e Johnny thinks Clara isn't very kind.
f Clara thinks Johnny is a great listener.

**3 1.62 Listen to Tom and Patsy and answer the questions.**

a How are Tom and Patsy related?
b How does Patsy feel about Tom?

**4 Listen again and underline the correct answers.**

a Patsy is **older** / **younger** than Tom.
b **Patsy** / **Tom** is not very fashionable.
c Patsy **always** / **never** buys clothes for Tom.
d Patsy **usually** / **never** watches sports on TV.
e Tom **likes** / **doesn't like** sitting in the backyard.
f Patsy thinks Tom is **very serious** / **very funny**.

## WRITING & SPEAKING

**1 Read the description. Check (✓) the questions that are answered.**

a What's his name?
b How are you related?
c What's the age difference between you?
d Do you have the same interests?
e Do you wear the same kinds of clothes?
f What does he do?
g Does he have any annoying habits?
h What are his best points?
i What do you think he's doing now?

### Me and my uncle

My uncle's name is David. He's my mother's youngest brother and he's only two years older than me. We're both students at the same college. David wants to work as an architect, whereas I want to be an engineer.

In many ways we are similar: we enjoy the same kind of music and we like the same kinds of movies.

However, there are some differences. David loves sports, but I prefer to play games on my computer. Another difference between us is the clothes we wear. I'm happy in jeans and a T-shirt, but David always wears designer pants, shirts, and shoes. The only thing I don't like about him is that he talks too much about fashion and not enough about important things.

On the other hand, David is the nicest person I know. When I have a problem, I know David is always ready to listen and give me good advice. We've both become closer over the last year, and I now think of David as a friend as well as my uncle.

**2 Find the words/phrases from the box in the text and underline them.**

both   but   however   on the other hand   whereas

**Complete the rules using the words/phrases in the box.**

**Expressing similarity**

a You use ___both___ when you want to say the same thing about two people or things.

**Expressing contrast**

b ___________ and ___________ are often used to contrast ideas within the same sentence.
c ___________ and ___________ are often used to contrast ideas in two different sentences.

**3 Underline the correct expressions in these sentences.**

a I like playing soccer. **However** / **Whereas**, my brother prefers tennis.
b I like playing soccer, **however** / **whereas** my brother prefers tennis.
c I can't stand watching sports. **But** / **On the other hand**, I love playing them.
d I can't stand watching sports, **but** / **on the other hand** I love playing them.

**4 Write the words in the correct order.**

a both / dancing / love / We
b have / both / We / the USA / to / been

**Work with a partner. Are the sentences true for you?**

**5 You're going to tell your partner about a member of your family and compare yourself with him/her.**

- Choose some questions in Exercise 1 that you can answer.
- Think about what you're going to say and the language you will need.
- When you're ready, take turns telling each other about a member of your family.

**6 Write a comparison between yourself and a member of your family. Try to answer as many of the questions in Exercise 1 as you can. Use the expressions in Exercise 2 to describe contrast and similarity.**

# Pairwork: Student A

## UNIT 1

**Ask Student B to describe the people in picture B. Their names are: James, Angela, Melinda, Joe, and Peter. Label picture B.**

Which one is Joe?

He has short, dark hair with blond highlights. He doesn't have a beard.

Kyle Tina Cathy Raymond Ann

1 _____ 2 _____ 3 _____ 4 _____ 5 _____

## UNIT 2

**Eight cities**

**You have eight maps of different countries (a–h).**

- Four cities are marked on maps (a–d). Describe to Student B exactly where these cities are.
- Student B will describe the locations of the other four cities (e–h). Mark them on your maps.
- Compare your maps with Student B.

Japan France South Korea Iceland Spain Egypt Australia Czech Republic

## UNIT 3

**What were you doing yesterday?**

**Find out if you were doing the same things at the same times as Student B yesterday.**

- Complete the sentences in the *Me* column describing what you were doing yesterday at those times.
- Ask Student B questions beginning with *What were ...?* and complete the *Student B* column.

What were you doing at 6:00 a.m.?

I was sleeping.

- Were you doing the same thing or different things?

| | Me | Student B | ✓ = Same thing<br>✖ = Different things |
|---|---|---|---|
| a | At 6:00 a.m. I was ________ | He/She was ________ | ________ |
| b | At 7:30 a.m. I was ________ | ________ | ________ |
| c | At 10:00 a.m. I was ________ | ________ | ________ |
| d | At 1:00 p.m. I was ________ | ________ | ________ |
| e | At 6:00 p.m. I was ________ | ________ | ________ |

## UNIT 4

### What's happening in your life?

**How much do you know about what's happening in Student B's life right now?**

- Write sentences in the affirmative or negative, according to what you think.
- Ask Student B questions to check if you were right or wrong.

Are you trying to eat less sugar? — Yes, I am. — I was right!

| Student B's name: ______________ | | ✓ = I was right! ✖ = I was wrong! |
|---|---|---|
| a try to eat less sugar | *He/She is trying to eat less sugar.* | ✓ |
| b write a book | ______________ | ______ |
| c apply for jobs | ______________ | ______ |
| d learn to dance | ______________ | ______ |
| e ______________ | ______________ | ______ |

## UNIT 5

### Trivia quiz

**You and Student B each have five trivia questions. You have the correct answers to Student B's questions in the box below. Student B has the correct answers to your questions.**

- Look at the trivia questions in the table and guess the answers.
- Complete the *My guess* column with your ideas.
- Ask Student B the questions and complete the *Correct answer* column.
- Compare your guesses with the correct answers. How good or bad were your guesses?

| Trivia questions | My guess | Correct answer |
|---|---|---|
| a How fast can a dolphin swim? | ______ | ______ |
| b How much money did J.K. Rowling (author of *Harry Potter*) earn in 2005? | ______ | ______ |
| c How many words does a woman speak in a normal day? | ______ | ______ |
| d What percentage of the body's energy does the brain use? | ______ | ______ |
| e What is the longest distance ever traveled in a wheelchair? | ______ | ______ |

**Answers to Student B's questions:**

105 km/h   $93,820,000   2,175   2%   4,203 km

## UNIT 6

### Experiences

**What experiences has Student B had?**

- Write Student B's name in the space below.
- Write statements (a-g) that you think are true.
- Write questions to check your statements.
- Ask Student B the questions.

| Student B's name: ______________ | | Questions | ✓ = I'm right! ✖ = I'm wrong! |
|---|---|---|---|
| a break his/her leg | *Ana has (never) broken her leg.* | *Have you ever broken your leg?* | ______ |
| b sing karaoke | ______________ | ______________ | ______ |
| c ride a motorcycle | ______________ | ______________ | ______ |
| d go fishing | ______________ | ______________ | ______ |
| e eat escargot | ______________ | ______________ | ______ |
| f buy a painting | ______________ | ______________ | ______ |
| g ______________ | ______________ | ______________ | ______ |

# Pairwork: Student B

## UNIT 1

**Ask Student A to describe the people in picture A. Their names are: Tina, Kyle, Cathy, Raymond and Ann. Label picture A.**

Which one is Cathy?

She has curly, blonde hair with blue eyes.

A

1 _____ 2 _____ 3 _____ 4 _____ 5 _____

B

Angela Melinda James Joe Peter

## UNIT 2

### Eight cities

**You have eight maps of different countries (a–h).**

- Four cities are marked on maps (e-h). Describe to Student A exactly where these cities are.
- Student A will describe the locations of the other four cities (a-d). Mark them on your maps.
- Compare your maps with Student A.

a

Japan

b
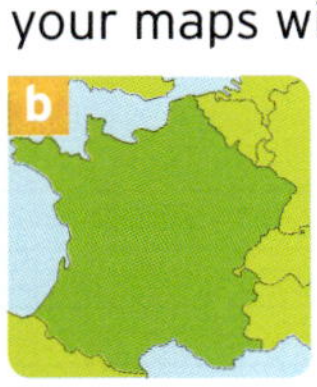
France

c

South Korea

d
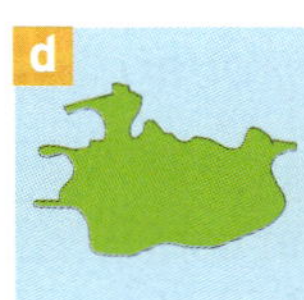
Iceland

e

Spain

f

Egypt

g

Australia

h

Czech Republic

## UNIT 3

### What were you doing yesterday?

**Find out if you were doing the same things at the same times as Student A yesterday.**

- Complete the sentences in the *Me* column describing what you were doing yesterday at those times.
- Ask Student A questions beginning with *What were …?* and complete the *Student A* column.

What were you doing at 6:00 a.m.?

I was sleeping.

- Were you doing the same thing or different things?

| | Me | Student A | ✓ = We were doing the same things<br>✖ = We were doing different things |
|---|---|---|---|
| a | At 6:00 a.m. I was _______ | He/She was ____________ | _______ |
| b | At 7:30 a.m. I was _______ | ____________ | _______ |
| c | At 10:00 a.m. I was _______ | ____________ | _______ |
| d | At 1:00 p.m. I was _______ | ____________ | _______ |
| e | At 6:00 p.m. I was _______ | ____________ | _______ |

## UNIT 4

### What's happening in your life?

**How much do you know about what's happening in Student A's life right now?**

- Write sentences in the affirmative or negative, according to what you think.
- Ask Student A questions to check if you were right or wrong.

Are you trying to do more exercise? | Yes, I am. | I was right!

| Student A's name: ______ | | ✓ = I was right! ✖ = I was wrong! |
|---|---|---|
| a try to do more exercise | *He/She is trying to do more exercise* | ✓ |
| b learn to drive | ______ | ______ |
| c plan a trip abroad | ______ | ______ |
| d read a good book | ______ | ______ |
| e ______ | ______ | ______ |

## UNIT 5

### Trivia quiz

**You and Student A each have five trivia questions. You have the correct answers to Student A's questions in the box below. Student A has the correct answers to your questions.**

- Look at the trivia questions in the table and guess the answers.
- Complete the *My guess* column with your ideas.
- Ask Student A the questions and complete the *Correct answer* column.
- Compare your guesses with the correct answers. How good or bad were your guesses?

| Trivia questions | My guess | Correct answer |
|---|---|---|
| a How fast can a cheetah run? | ______ | ______ |
| b How much money did Dan Brown (author of *The Da Vinci Code*) earn in 2005? | ______ | ______ |
| c How many words does a man speak in a normal day? | ______ | ______ |
| d What percentage of the body's weight is the brain? | ______ | ______ |
| e What is the longest distance ever traveled on a windsurf board? | ______ | ______ |

**Answers to Student A's questions:**

30 km/h    $80,137,000    7,120    20%    40,075.16 km

## UNIT 6

### Experiences

**What experiences has Student A had?**

- Write Student A's name in the space below.
- Write statements (a–g) that you think are true.
- Write questions to check your statements.
- Ask Student A the questions.

| Student A's name: ______ | | Questions | ✓ = I'm right! ✖ = I'm wrong! |
|---|---|---|---|
| a go to Canada | *Jan has (never) been to Canada.* | *Have you ever been to Canada?* | ______ |
| b give a speech | ______ | ______ | ______ |
| c break the speed limit | ______ | ______ | ______ |
| d cut somebody's hair | ______ | ______ | ______ |
| e cry at the movies | ______ | ______ | ______ |
| f forget his/her mother's birthday | ______ | ______ | ______ |
| g ______ | ______ | ______ | ______ |

# Grammar Extra

## UNIT 1: Questions. Tense review

### Questions

**Word order**

The usual word order for questions is:

| Question word | (Auxiliary) verb | Subject | |
|---|---|---|---|
| - | Is | she | happy? |
| - | Have | they | eaten? |
| What | does | "niece" | mean? |
| Where | are | you | going? |
| When | did | he | graduate? |

**Yes/No questions and short answers**

In *Yes/No* questions with *be*, you put *am/are/is/was/were* before the subject.
***Is** she tired? Yes, she is.*
***Were** they late? No, they weren't.*

In *Yes/No* questions with the simple present and the simple past, you put *do/does/did* before the subject.
***Do** you live here? Yes, I do.*
***Did** Jim and his two sisters go to college? No, they didn't.*

In *Yes/No* questions with other verb structures, you put the auxiliary verb before the subject.
***Have** you been to Peru? Yes, I have.*
***Can** she drive? No, she can't.*

**Wh questions**

Questions with *What, Where, How many,* etc. have the same word order as *Yes/No* questions.
You put a question word at the beginning of the question.
***Why** is she tired?*
***Where** do you live?*
***How** many times have you been to Peru?*

### Tense review

| Tense | Uses | Affirmative | Negative | Question |
|---|---|---|---|---|
| Simple present | facts/habits/routines | He **works**. | He **doesn't** work. | **Does** he **work**? |
| Simple past | completed action at a specific past time | She **worked** yesterday. | She **didn't work** yesterday. | **Did** she **work** yesterday? |
| Present progressive | activities in progress now | They**'re working** now. | They **aren't working** now. | **Are** they **working** now? |
| Future with (*be*) *going to* | future plans and intentions | We**'re going to work** tomorrow. | We **aren't going to work tomorrow**. | **Are** we **going to work tomorrow?** |
| Present perfect | completed action in "time up to now" | It's **worked** recently. | It **hasn't worked** recently. | **Has** it **worked** recently? |

## UNIT 1: Exercises

**1 Write *Yes/No* questions with *you*.**

Somebody wants to know if you ...

a like jazz *Do you like jazz?*
b can swim
c went skiing last winter
d are wearing jeans today
e have been to Argentina
f are going to drive home after the class

**2 Write short answers to the questions in Exercise 1.**

a Yes, I do. / No, I don't.

**Check (✓) the short answer that is true for you.**

**3 Think of a person you know well. Use the information in Exercise 1 and write *Yes/No* questions and short answers with *he* or *she*.**

a Does he like jazz?
Yes, he does. / No, he doesn't.

**Check (✓) the short answer that is true (if you know it).**

**4 Insert the subject *you* in the correct position to make questions.**

a How far do live from the school?
*How far do you live from the school?*
b When did last go to the theater?
c What are going to do this evening?
d How many cups of coffee have had today?
e What kind of pen are using right now?
f Where did buy your shoes?

**Ask your partner the questions.**

**5 Complete the questions with *you* and then match the questions and the answers.**

a What / do? *What do you do?* — 3
b Who / work for?
c Which department / work in?
d How / get to work?
e When / start working there?
f Why / like working there?
g How much / earn?

1 In 2005.
2 On foot.
3 I'm a computer programmer.
4 Because I love computer games.
5 In the games department.
6 $63,000 a year.
7 Microsoft.

**Write your own answers to the questions.**

**6 Name the tense for each sentence.**

a We're studying Shakespeare in our English class. *Present progressive.*
b My parents named me after my uncle.
c I've recently learned to drive.
d My friends are going to organize a party for me tomorrow.
e I like getting up early in the morning.

**Put each sentence into the negative.**

a *We aren't studying Shakespeare in our English class.*

**Check (✓) the sentences (affirmative or negative) that are true for you.**

a *We're studying Shakespeare in our English class.* ✓

## UNIT 2: Nouns and quantity expressions

### Countable nouns

Most nouns in English are countable. They have a singular and a plural form.

**Regular forms**

| **Singular** | **Plural** | **Spelling** |
|---|---|---|
| a place | two places | Add **s**. |
| a church | three churches | Add **es** after *ch*, *sh*, *s*, *x*. |
| a city | ten cities | Add **ies** after a consonant + *y*. |

**Irregular forms**

| **Singular** | **Plural** |
|---|---|
| a person | two people |
| a child | two children |
| a man | two men |
| a woman | two women |

**a or an?**

With singular nouns, you use *a* before a consonant sound: ***a** town*, ***a** college*.
You use *an* before a vowel sound: ***an** airport*, ***an** office*.

**Plural nouns**

Some nouns are always plural and don't have a singular form. You can't use *a/an* or put a number in front of them.
*I have **some** pink jeans.* (NOT ~~*I have a pink jeans.*~~)
Common plural nouns: *clothes*, *glasses*, *jeans*, *pajamas*, *pants*, *scissors*, *shorts*, *sunglasses*.

### Uncountable nouns

Some nouns in English are uncountable. They only have a singular form. You can't use *a/an* or put a number in front of them.
*We had bad weather.* (NOT ~~*We had a bad weather.*~~)
Common uncountable nouns: *advice*, *architecture*, *food*, *furniture*, *homework*, *information*, *knowledge*, *love*, *money*, *music*, *news*, *traffic*, *transportation*, *weather*, *work*.

### Quantity expressions

These are ways you can talk about quantity if you can't or don't want to use an exact number.
With countable nouns: (*only*) *a few* / (*way*) *too many* / *How many ...?*
*Only **a few** people saw what happened.*
***How many** emails do you get every day?*

With uncountable nouns: (*only*) *a little* / (*way*) *too much* / *How much ...?*
*There's **a little** juice left, but no water.*
***How much** homework do you get?*

With countable and uncountable nouns: *a lot of* / *lots of* / *not ... enough*
*She has **a lot of** problems.*
*He did**n't** give me **enough** information.*

*too* + *much/many* (+ noun) = excessive or more than necessary.
*I have **too much** work and not enough time.*

## UNIT 2: Exercises

**1 Write the plural forms for the following countable nouns.**

a a name *names*
b a place
c a menu
d a bus
e a family
f a wife
g a person
h a foot
i a day
j a mouse
k a camera
l a watch

**2 Put the nouns in the box into the table.**

advice child city homework information money news office problem tooth weather woman

| Countable nouns | Uncountable nouns |
|---|---|
| *child* | *advice* |
| | |
| | |
| | |
| | |

**Add three more nouns to each column.**

**3 Complete the sentences with *a/an* or *some*.**

a I have *some* money in my pocket.
b I have ______ gold ring on my finger.
c I have ______ black jeans at home.
d I have ______ scissors in my bag.
e I have ______ homework to do this evening.
f I have ______ laptop I use for work.
g I have ______ great music on my phone.
h I have ______ sunglasses in my car.

**Check (✓) the sentences that are true for you.**

**4 Underline the correct form of *be*.**

a How **is** / **are** the weather today?
b How **was** / **were** the traffic this morning?
c What **is** / **are** the people like on your street?
d What **is** / **are** the furniture like in your living room?
e What **was** / **were** the English teachers like at your high school?
f What **was** / **were** the food like at the last restaurant you went to?

**Ask your partner the questions.**

**5 Complete the sentences with *be* + *a lot of*.**

In my city ...

a there *are a lot of* parks.
b there ____________ good nightlife.
c there ____________ good restaurants.
d there ______ traffic.
e there ______ pollution.
f there ______ bookstores.

**Make the sentences negative. Use *not be* + *much/many*.**

a There aren't many parks.

**Which sentences are true for your city?**

**6 Look at Paul. What do you think is wrong with his lifestyle? Write sentences with *too much/many* and *not enough*.**

a drink / beer
*He drinks too much beer.*
b eat / pizzas
c eat / fruit and vegetables
d smoke / cigarettes
e do / exercise
f watch / TV
g get / fresh air

## UNIT 3: Simple past. Past progressive

### Part 1: Simple past

| Affirmative | Negative | Question | Short answer *Yes* | Short answer *No* |
|---|---|---|---|---|
| I/You/He/She/It/ We/They **worked.** | I/You/He/She/It/ We/They **didn't (did not) worked.** | Did I/you/he/she/it/ we/they **work**? | Yes, I/you/he/she/ it/we/they **did**. | No, I/you/he/she/it/ we/they **didn't**. |

**Spelling: regular verbs**

Add *ed/d* after most verbs: work – work**ed**; demonstrate – demonstrate**d**.
Delete *y* and add *ied* for verbs that end in a consonant + *y*: study – stud**ied**; try – tr**ied**.
Add a consonant + *ed* for verbs that end in one vowel + one consonant: stop – stop**ped**; plan – plan**ned**.

The ten most frequently used irregular verbs are:

1 say – said
2 get – got
3 go – went
4 know – knew
5 think – thought
6 see – saw
7 make – made
8 come – came
9 take – took
10 give – gave

You can use the simple past as the main tense to talk about past events and past situations. It's commonly used to tell stories.

⚠ There is only one past form for every verb except *be*.

| Affirmative | Negative | Question | Short answer *Yes* | Short answer *No* |
|---|---|---|---|---|
| I/He/She/It **was** tired. | I/He/She/It **wasn't** (**was not**) tired. | **Was** I/he/she/it tired? | Yes, I/you/he/she/ it **was**. | No, I/you/he/she/it **wasn't**. |
| You/We/They **were** tired. | You/we/they **weren't** (**were not**) tired. | **Were** you/we/ they tired? | Yes, you/we/they **were**. | No, you/we/they **weren't**. |

### Part 2: Past progressive

| Affirmative | Negative | Question | Short answer *Yes* | Short answer *No* |
|---|---|---|---|---|
| I/He/She/It **was working**. | I/He/She/It **wasn't** (**was not**) **working**. | **Was** I/he/she/it **working**? | Yes, I/you/he/she/ it **was**. | No, I/you/he/she/it **wasn't**. |
| You/We/They **were working**. | You/we/they **weren't** (**were not**) **working**. | **Were** you/we/ they **working**? | Yes, you/we/they **were**. | No, you/we/they **weren't**. |

**Spelling: *ing* forms**

Delete *e* and add *ing* for verbs that end in e: have – hav**ing**; make – mak**ing**
Add a consonant + *ing* for verbs that end in one vowel + one consonant: run – run**ning**; stop – stop**ping**

You can use the past progressive to describe a "longer" activity that was in progress when other past events happened. You usually use it in contrast with the simple past.
*I saw her when I **was driving** home.*
*They **were playing** tennis when it started raining.*

## UNIT 3: Exercises

### Part 1: Simple past

**1 Write the simple past forms for these verb sets.**

a work *worked* / go / call / help
b take / make / wake / bake
c try / play / study / copy
d stop / plan / hop / walk

**In each set, which verb doesn't belong? Why?**

a *"go – went" doesn't belong because it's irregular.*

**2 Write the simple past forms of these irregular verbs.**

a teach *taught*
b sit
c say
d know
e speak
f make
g begin
h ring
i fall
j learn
k catch
l fly
m sink
n throw
o swim
p read
q understand
r bring
s run
t sleep
u find
v wear
w buy
x come
y meet
z think

**3 Use the prompts in parentheses to write negative sentences about the past.**

a My father taught me how to swim. (how to drive)
*My father didn't teach me how to drive.*
b I went to a public school. (private school)
c My parents gave me money for my birthday. (a gift)
d I had fish for dinner last night. (meat)
e I studied French at school. (English)
f I played tennis when I was young. (basketball)

**Check (✓) the sentences that are true for you.**

### Part 2: Past progressive

**1 Write the *ing* form of these verbs.**

a come *coming*
b eat
c hit
d leave
e play
f put
g stay
h study
i swim
j wake
k win
l work

**2 Complete the questions and short answers about these times yesterday.**

a 8:00 a.m. Were you having breakfast? Yes, I was. No, I wasn't.
b 8:30 a.m. Were you driving to work? Yes, I ______. No, I ______.
c 10:00 a.m. ______ your mother working? Yes, she ______. No, she ______.
d 4:00 p.m. ______ you walking around town? Yes, I ______. No, I ______.
e 8:00 p.m. ______ your parents watching TV? Yes, they ______. No, they ______.

**Ask your partner the questions.**

**3 Complete the sentences with the simple past or the past progressive.**

a We (move) ___*moved*___ several times when I was a child.
b My parents met when they (study) ______ at college.
c When I finished school, I (start) ______ work in a bank.
d When I looked out of the window this morning, it (rain) ______.
e When I got to work, I (turn on) ______ my computer.
f When the teacher came into the classroom, I (talk) ______ to my friend on my cell phone.

**Check (✓) the sentences that are true for you.**

## UNIT 4: Verb patterns. Simple present and present progressive

### Part 1: Verb patterns – verbs with two objects

Some common verbs can have two objects. Two different word orders are possible, but the meaning is the same. The word order **verb + person + thing** is more common, especially with object pronouns (*me, you, him*, etc.).

| | | indirect object | direct object | | | | direct object | indirect object | |
|---|---|---|---|---|---|---|---|---|---|
| | **verb** + | **person** + | **thing** | = | | **verb** + | **thing** + | ***to/for*** + | **person** |
| I | bought | him | a gift. | = | I | bought | a gift | for | him. |
| He | lent | her | some money | = | He | lent | some money | to | her. |

Common verbs with the pattern **verb** + **thing** + ***to*** + **person**: *give, lend, offer, pass, read, send, show, teach, tell.*
Common verbs with the pattern **verb** + **thing** + ***for*** + **person**: *buy, find, get, make.*

⚠ You can't use the word order **verb** + **person** + **thing** with certain verbs: e.g. *describe, explain, say*, or *suggest.*
*He explained the situation to me.* (NOT ~~He explained me the situation.~~)
*She said hello to us.* (NOT ~~She said us hello.~~)

---

### Part 2: Simple present and present progressive

**Simple present**

| Affirmative | Negative | Question | Short answer *Yes* | Short answer *No* |
|---|---|---|---|---|
| I/You/We/They **work.** | I/You/We/They **don't** (**do not**) **work.** | **Do** I/we/they **work**? | Yes, I/we/they **do.** | No, I/you/we/they **don't.** |
| He/She/It **works.** | He/She/It **doesn't** (**does not**) **work.** | **Does** he/she/it **work**? | Yes, he/she/it **does.** | No, he/she/it **doesn't.** |

**Spelling: 3rd person singular**

Add *s* after most verbs: live – live**s**; play – play**s**; work – work**s**
Add *es* after *ch, sh, s, x*: watch – watch**es**; finish – finish**es**
Delete *y* and add *ies* after a consonant + *y*: study – stud**ies**
Irregular forms: do – **does**; go – **goes**; have – **has**

You can use the simple present to talk about:

- things that are always true. *He looks like his father. Ice forms at 0 ºC.*
- things that happen regularly or all the time. *He plays tennis on Friday.*
  *She never gets up before 9:00 a.m.*

**Present progressive**

| Affirmative | Negative | Question | Short answer *Yes* | Short answer *No* |
|---|---|---|---|---|
| **I'm** (**am**) **working.** | **I'm not** (**am not**) **working.** | **Am** I **working**? | Yes, I **am.** | No, **I'm not.** |
| You/We/They**'re** (**are**) **working.** | You/We/They **aren't** (**are not**) **working.** | **Are** you/we/they **working**? | Yes, you/we/they **are.** | No, you/we/they **aren't.** |
| He/She/It**'s** (**is**) **working.** | He/She/It **isn't** (**is not**) **working.** | **Is** he/she/it **working**? | Yes, he/she/it **is.** | No, he/she/it **isn't.** |

**Spelling: *ing* forms**

Delete *e* and add *ing* for verbs that end in *e*: have – hav**ing**; make – mak**ing**
Add a consonant + *ing* for verbs that end in one vowel + one consonant: run – run**ning**; stop – stop**ping**
You can use the present progressive to talk about:

- activities that are in progress at the moment of speaking. *What are you **doing**? I'm **writing** an email.*
- activities that are in progress around the moment of speaking.
  *Cars are **getting** cheaper, but house prices are **going up**.*

## UNIT 4: Exercises

### Part 1: Verb patterns – verbs with two objects

**1 Complete the sentences about last Christmas.**

a Anna: some socks ⟶ Grandpa
*Anna gave Grandpa some socks.*
b John: a cell phone ⟶ Tony
c Dick: some chocolate ⟶ Molly
d Sue: a cook book ⟶ Carlos
e Becky: a DVD ⟶ Eric
f Jimmy: some earrings ⟶ Sally

**What gifts did you give people last year?** *I gave my mom a foot spa.*

**2 Underline the appropriate prepositions.**

a Could you send the money **for** / **to** me?
b She explained the rules **for** / **to** them.
c My dad bought this **for** / **to** me for my birthday.
d I've told that joke **for** / **to** everybody!
e He described the house **for** / **to** her.
f We showed pictures of our vacation **for** / **to** him.
g Ian is getting some ice cream **for** / **to** us.
h They didn't say goodbye **for** / **to** us.
i I don't have time to make breakfast **for** / **to** him!
j Can you lend your bike **for** / **to** Sue?

**3 Re-read the sentences in Exercise 2. Where possible, change the word order and rewrite the sentences without the prepositions.**

a *Could you send me the money?*
b *(Not possible to change.)*

---

### Part 2: Simple present and present progressive

**1 Write these verbs in the simple present 3rd person singular.**

a be *is*
b cry
c do
d go
e have
f hear
g pay
h push
i say
j study
k take
l touch

**2 Write the *ing* form of these verbs.**

a become *becoming*
b choose
c cut
d fly
e live
f meet
g shine
h shut
i sit
j start
k stay
l wear

**3 Write a question in the simple present and a question in the present progressive for each prompt.**

a you / wear / perfume?
*Do you wear perfume?*
*Are you wearing perfume?*
b you / use / an electronic dictionary?
c you / plan / your vacations?
d your parents / work?
e your teacher / wear / glasses?
f What / you / do?

**Answer the questions. Think about the difference in meaning for each question.**

**4 Complete the questions with *you* in the most appropriate tense: simple present or present progressive.**

a Where / come from? *Where do you come from?*
b How many languages / speak?
c What / wear today?
d Why / learn English?
e What time / usually go to bed?
f What color pen / use to do this exercise?

**Answer the questions.**

## UNIT 5: Comparative and superlative adjectives. Phrasal verbs

### Part 1: Comparative and superlative adjectives

| | Adjective | Comparative | Superlative |
|---|---|---|---|
| **Short adjectives: add *er/est*** | | | |
| Adjectives ending in a consonant or *e* | new | new**er** | the new**est** |
| | nice | nice**r** | the nic**est** |
| Adjectives ending in a single vowel + a single consonant | big | bigg**er** | the bigg**est** |
| Adjectives ending in *y* | healthy | health**ier** | the health**iest** |
| **Irregular adjectives** | good | better | the best |
| | bad | worse | the worst |
| **Long adjectives: add *more/the most*** | exciting | **more** exciting | **the most** exciting |

You use comparative adjectives to compare people/things with other people/things.
*Fernando Alonso is* ***older than*** *Lewis Hamilton.*
You can use *a little bit* or *much* to modify comparisons.
*Olímpico Stadium is* ***a little bit bigger than*** *the Jalisco Stadium.*

You use *not as* + adjective + *as* to make negative comparisons.
*Golf is* ***not as dangerous as*** *motor racing.*
You use superlative adjectives to compare people/things with all the other people/things in their group.
*Muhammad Ali is* ***the greatest*** *sportsman of all time.*
*Soccer is* ***the most popular*** *sport in the world.*

### Part 2: Phrasal verbs

The term "phrasal verb" usually refers to all multi-word verbs, consisting of a verb + particle(s). Phrasal verbs can be divided into three basic types.

1 **Verb + particle (INTRANSITIVE)**
Some phrasal verbs are intransitive and don't take a direct object.
***Sit down*** *and enjoy it.*
*When are you going to* ***grow up****?*

2 **Verb + object + particle (TRANSITIVE – SEPARABLE)**
The biggest group of phrasal verbs is transitive. These verbs take a direct object. With separable verbs, when the direct object is a noun, you can put it before or after the particle.
***Take off*** *your shoes.* OR ***Take*** *your shoes* ***off.***
When the direct object is a pronoun, you have to put it between the verb and the particle.
***Turn*** *it* ***off****, please.* (NOT ~~*Turn off it*~~.)

3 **Verb + particle + object (TRANSITIVE – NOT SEPARABLE)**
With this type of phrasal verb, you always put the direct object – noun or pronoun – after the particle.
*She* ***takes care*** *of her grandmother.*
*I* ***ran after*** *the bus, but it didn't stop.*

# UNIT 5: Exercises

## Comparative and superlative adjectives

**1 Complete the table with the adjectives in the box.**

~~bad~~ ~~famous~~ good ~~happy~~ interesting ~~kind~~ lazy lucky nice ~~sad~~ strong successful thin wet

| | | |
|---|---|---|
| a | Add *er/r* | kind — kinder than |
| b | Double letter + *er* | sad — sadder than |
| c | Delete *y*, add *ier* | happy — happier than |
| d | Irregular | bad — worse than |
| e | *more* + adjective | famous — more famous than |

**2 Write sentences comparing the places. Use *a little bit* or *much* and the comparative form of the adjective.**

a France / big / Spain
France is a little bit bigger than Spain.
b India / hot / Canada
c The Nile River / long / the Amazon
d Tokyo / expensive / Bangkok
e Rome / far north / Barcelona
f Manila / crowded / Helsinki

**Rewrite the sentences using *not as ... as* so they have the same meaning.**

a Spain isn't as big as France.

**3 Use *a little bit* / *much* / *not as ... as* to write true sentences comparing the following. Use the adjectives in the box or your own ideas.**

complicated confident difficult energetic expensive healthy large modern old sophisticated

a your mom / your dad
My mom is a little bit older than my dad.
b English / your language
c you ten years ago / you now
d your first cell phone / the cell phone you have now
e the house you were born in / the house you live in now
f your town ten years ago / your town now

**Compare your sentences with a partner.**

## Part 2: Phrasal verbs

**1 Rewrite these sentences so that they have the same meaning.**

a Can you turn off the light, please?
Can you turn the light off, please?
b She threw my letter away.
c I'd like to try on this dress, please.
d Pick all the papers up before you leave!
e Write down your name, please.
f I gave back his pen.

**2 Put the words in parentheses in the correct order to complete each sentence. Consult your dictionary if necessary.**

a I'm very similar to my mother – I take after her. (after / take / her)
b I have good relationships with my neighbors – I ________________. (get / well / them / with / along)
c I keep my neighbors' pet when they go on vacation – I ________________. (take care / it / of)
d I lived with my grandparents when I was a child – they ________________. (up / brought / me)
e My children always leave their things on the floor – they don't ________________. (away / them / put)
f I invent stories for my kids - they love them! I ________________. (make / up / them)
g I stopped going to the gym – I ________________. (up / it / gave)
h When I see a new phrasal verb, I consult my dictionary – I ________________. (it / look / up)

**Are any of the sentences true for you?**

## UNIT 6: Permission and obligation (present). Present perfect

### Part 1: *can* for permission; *have to* for obligation

| Affirmative | Negative | Question | Short answer *Yes* | Short answer *No* |
|---|---|---|---|---|
| I/You/He, *etc.* **can work.** | I/You/He, *etc.* **can't** (**cannot**) **work.** | **Can** I/you/he, *etc.* **work**? | Yes, I/you/he, *etc.* **can.** | No, I/you/he, *etc.* **can't.** |

You can use *can* and *can't* to talk about permission.

- *Can* means something is permitted: it's OK.
  *In my country, you* ***can*** *leave school when you are sixteen.*
- *Can't* means something isn't permitted: it isn't OK.
  *You* ***can't*** *vote until you are eighteen.*

| Affirmative | Negative | Question | Short answer *Yes* | Short answer *No* |
|---|---|---|---|---|
| I/You/We/They **have to work.** | I/You/We/They **don't have to work.** | Do I/you/we/they **have to work**? | Yes, I/you/we/they **do.** | No, I/you/we/they **don't.** |
| He/She/It **has to work.** | He/She/It **doesn't have to work.** | Does he/she/it **have to work**? | Yes, he/she/it **does.** | No, he/she/it **doesn't.** |

You use *have to / don't have to* to talk about necessity or obligation.

- *Have to* means something is necessary or it's obligatory.
  *In the USA, you* ***have to*** *drive on the right.*
- *Don't have to* means something isn't necessary or it isn't obligatory.
  *You* ***don't have to*** *wear a helmet on a bicycle.*

---

### Part 2: Present perfect

| Affirmative | Negative | Question | Short answer *Yes* | Short answer *No* |
|---|---|---|---|---|
| I/You/We/They've (**have**) **worked.** | I/You/We/They **haven't** (**have not**) **worked.** | **Have** I/you/we/they **worked**? | Yes, I/you/we/they **have.** | No, I/you/we/they **haven't.** |
| He/She/It's (**has**) **worked.** | He/She/It **hasn't** (**has not**) **worked.** | **Has** he/she/it **worked**? | Yes, he/she/it **has.** | No, he/she/it **hasn't.** |

You can use the present perfect to talk about completed actions in time "up to now." You don't focus on when.

**Time "up to now"**

Common time expressions which describe time "up to now": *today, this week, recently, never, over the years.*
With these time expressions, you usually use the present perfect.

*My brother* ***has never been*** *to a rock concert.*
*I* ***haven't seen*** *any good movies* ***recently.***

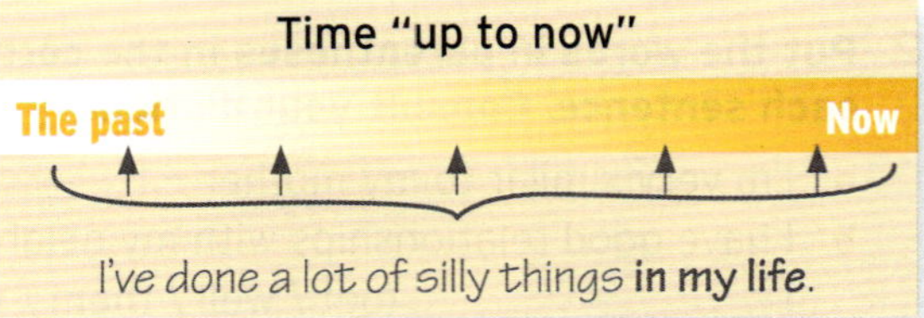


⚠ ***been*** is the past participle of ***be***, but you can also use it as a past participle of ***go***. Compare:

- *He's* ***been*** *to Rome.* = He went and came back.
- *He's* ***gone*** *to Rome.* = He went and is in Rome now.

**"Finished" time**

Common time expressions which describe "finished" time: *yesterday, last month, in 1990, a few minutes ago.*
With these time expressions, you use the simple past.

*She* ***called*** *you* ***a few minutes ago.***
*I* ***didn't go*** *to the mountains* ***last summer.***

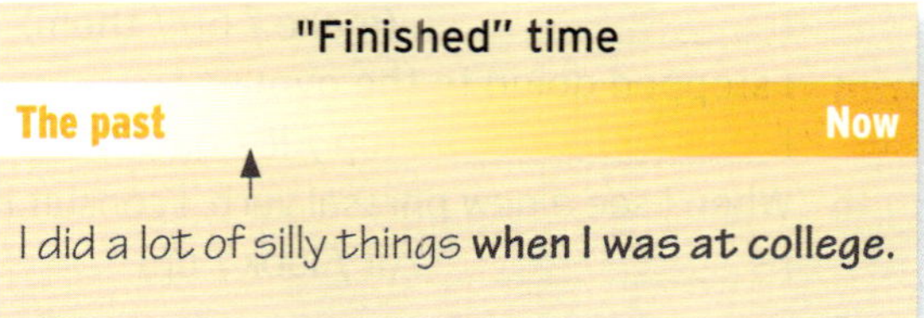

## UNIT 6: Exercises

### Part 1: *can* for permission; *have to* for obligation

**1 Work with a partner. Test your knowledge of life in Texas. Underline the correct verbs in these sentences.**

- a You **have to** / **can** leave school when you're sixteen.
- b You **don't have to** / **can't** wear a helmet on a bicycle but it is safer if you do.
- c You **have to** / **can** vote when you're eighteen.
- d You **don't have to** / **can't** go to college unless you want to.
- e You **have to** / **can** fly an airplane when you're twenty-one.
- f You **have to** / **can** drive on the right.
- g You **have to** / **can** drive a car when you're sixteen.
- h You **don't have to** / **can't** carry an ID card.

**Check (✓) the sentences that are true for your country.**

**2 Write similar sentences about the things you can, can't, have to, or don't have to do in your country.**

---

### Part 2: Present perfect

**1 Complete the tables with the correct past participles for these irregular verbs.**

| Infinitive | Simple past | Past participle |
|---|---|---|
| be | was/were | 1 *been* |
| do | did | 2 ______ |
| take | took | 3 ______ |
| drink | drank | 4 ______ |
| break | broke | 5 ______ |
| see | saw | 6 ______ |
| eat | ate | 7 ______ |
| write | wrote | 8 ______ |
| forget | forgot | 9 ______ |
| ride | rode | 10 ______ |
| become | became | 11 ______ |
| stand | stood | 12 ______ |
| give | gave | 13 ______ |
| go | went | 14 *gone* / 15 ______ |

**2 Write the sentences in the negative.**

- a I've been on TV. *I haven't been on TV.*
- b I've sung karaoke.
- c I've driven a sports car.
- d I've met a famous person.
- e I've climbed a mountain.
- f I've called up a TV show.

**Check (✓) the sentences that are true for you.**

**3 Write present perfect questions with *you* for the sentences in Exercise 2.**

- a *Have you been on TV?*

**Ask your partner the questions.**

**4 Underline the correct tense.**

- a **I've never been** / **never went** to Australia.
- b I **haven't done** / **didn't do** my homework last night.
- c My parents **haven't called** / **didn't call** me recently.
- d **I've never eaten** / **didn't eat** sushi.
- e **I've been** / **went** skiing last winter.
- f **I've had** / **had** a bicycle when I was a child.

**Check (✓) the sentences that are true for you.**

# Audioscript

## Unit 1

1.02

**(M = Maria; B = Ben)**

**M:** Hi, I'm Maria.
**B:** Hi, Maria. My name's Benjamin, but nobody calls me Benjamin. Well, my parents do, but my friends call me Ben.
**M:** Ben – that's nice.
**B:** Thanks. Actually, my old friends call me Tree.
**M:** Tree? Why?
**B:** Well, as you can see, I'm very tall.
**M:** Oh, ha-ha. ... My friends call me lots of different names.
**B:** Really?
**M:** Yes. My mom's Mexican and my dad's English, so I've got English and Mexican friends, and they call me different things.
**B:** What do your Mexican friends call you?
**M:** They use my full name – Anna-Maria.
**B:** And your English friends?
**M:** They just call me Maria. Some of them call me Mimi.
**B:** Mimi! That's cute!
**M:** Well, it could be worse. My brother calls me Baby, because I'm the youngest in the family.
**B:** That's not so bad – my sisters call me Big Ben.
**M:** Ha-ha. Oh, no!

1.06

**1** Frank
**2** Tina
**3** Bobby
**4** Margaret
**5** Toby
**6** Anita
**7** Todd
**8** Georgina
**9** Karen

1.07

**a** Toby (5) has a shaved head. He's very good-looking.
**b** Georgina (8) has short, straight hair with blond highlights.
**c** Todd (7) has dark hair and green eyes.
**d** Bobby (3) has short, gray hair.
**e** Anita (6) has dark brown eyes and long hair.
**f** Margaret (4) has long, blonde hair. She's very cute.
**g** Tina (2) has long, red hair. She has a beautiful smile.
**h** Karen (9) has dark, curly hair.
**i** Frank (1) has gray hair and a gray beard.

1.09

John Carter is my best friend. We met when we were five years old, because our parents were friends and we went to the same school. He lives in Los Angeles now – he's a teacher at a high school there. So I only see him in the summer when he comes home to visit his family. Of course, we stay in touch by email and phone. He's important to me because he knows me so well. When I'm feeling down or when I need to talk to somebody, I can always call him. Recently, I had girlfriend problems and he was great. I'd say his best quality is that he's a really good listener. He just lets you talk and he listens. But he isn't perfect! He's always late for everything and he never says sorry. Never! One day last summer, we arranged to meet at seven o'clock to play baseball, and he arrived at nine thirty! It was almost dark! Oh well, nobody's perfect, are they? Last time I saw him was on my birthday, and we had a great time. We always have a great time.

1.10

**(A = Adam; B = Beth)**

**A:** Did you have a good weekend?
**B:** Not bad. How about you?
**A:** I had a really good dinner on Saturday night.
**B:** Oh.
**A:** Yes, we went to a new place in town – Edamame.
**B:** Ah.
**A:** They have a Japanese chef from Tokyo.
**B:** Uh-huh.
**A:** And the food is fantastic – they make their own sushi.
**B:** Oh.
**A:** Yes. It's the best sushi I've ever tasted.
**B:** Mm.
**A:** And it wasn't expensive. We had appetizers, an entrée, dessert, and coffee, and it only cost $25 each.
**B:** Ah.
**A:** I know. Unfortunately, when we got back to the car, we had a parking ticket.
**B:** Oh.

1.11

**(A = Adam; B = Beth)**

**A:** Did you have a good weekend?
**B:** Not bad. How about you?
**A:** I had a really good dinner on Saturday night.
**B:** Really?
**A:** Yes, we went to a new place in town – Edamame.
**B:** I've never heard of it.
**A:** They have a Japanese chef from Tokyo.
**B:** That sounds interesting.
**A:** And the food is fantastic – they make their own sushi.
**B:** Do they?
**A:** Yes. It's the best sushi I've ever tasted.
**B:** That sounds great.
**A:** And it wasn't expensive. We had appetizers, an entrée, dessert, and coffee, and it only cost $25 each.
**B:** Wow! That's great.
**A:** I know. Unfortunately, when we got back to the car, we had a parking ticket.
**B:** Oh, no! That's terrible.

1.13

**a** I'm Rei. I'm Japanese. My name means "beautiful".
**b** I'm Virat. My name means "brilliant". I'm from India.
**c** I'm Abeda from Ethiopia. My name means "flower".
**d** I'm from Mexico and my name is Ana, which means "grace".
**e** I'm Bjorn from Sweden. My name means "bear".
**f** I'm French. I'm Fabrice. My name means "craftsman."
**g** I'm Hai from China. My name means "ocean."
**h** I'm Dieter. My name means "warrior." I'm from Germany.

## Unit 2

1.15

**(I = Interviewer; P = Paulo; A = Armelle; L = Luigi)**

**Paulo**

**I:** Do you like your city?
**P:** Oh, yes, I feel lucky to be living in a city that's so big and exciting.
**I:** What's the architecture like?
**P:** A mixture of old and new. There are too many high-rise buildings in some parts of the city. But there are plenty of cheap restaurants and interesting cafés and bars. And the nightlife is great. We also have the most famous beach in the world – Copacabana Beach.
**I:** Ah. What's the weather like?
**P:** It's great most of the time. The only time I don't like Rio very much is in the summer: it's too hot and humid.

**Armelle**

**I:** Where do you live?
**A:** Well, I live in a small village with my parents. My grandparents live here too, and my aunts and uncles. In fact, I think I'm related to about fifty percent of the people in my village.
**I:** What's your village like?
**A:** It's very pretty. The countryside is beautiful, and the air is fresh and clean. But at night it's too quiet. I find it so dull and boring here – there aren't any discos or movie theaters.
**I:** What are the people like?
**A:** Oh, they're nice and really friendly, but there aren't many young people. I want to go and live in the city. Soon.

**Luigi**

**I:** What do you think of your city?
**L:** It is a very special place. It's such a romantic city.
**I:** What's it like downtown?
**L:** The buildings are beautiful, and we have San Marco, one of the most famous churches in the world. The Piazza San Marco is wonderful, and during carnival in February, Venice is the best place in the world to be.
**I:** Do you like living here?
**L:** No, I really hate living here. It's horrible. There are too many tourists everywhere. It gets very noisy and crowded.
**I:** Oh, no. What are the stores like?
**L:** Well, because of the tourists the stores are too expensive, and the canals are so dirty and polluted. My city is too small for all these people. Why don't they leave us in peace?

1.16

**A** Cuba – Cuban
Mexico – Mexican
Brazil – Brazilian
Argentina – Argentinian
**B** Egypt – Egyptian
Italy – Italian
Hungary – Hungarian
Canada – Canadian
**C** China – Chinese
Vietnam – Vietnamese
Portugal – Portuguese
Japan – Japanese

1.17

The best place I've ever visited is Buenos Aires, the capital of Argentina. It's a crazy city, but I really love it. The first time I went there was on my summer vacation. It was the year before I went to college. So I was young and excited, and it was my first time in South America. I flew there on my own, but I went to stay with friends. Of course, I visited all the tourist places - the Colon Theater, the Plaza de Mayo, La Boca, and my friends took me to watch a tango show. That was great. I even took some tango lessons, but I'm not very good. I also went out dancing a lot - Buenos Aires' nightlife is fantastic. The streets are crowded at three o'clock in the morning with people going to restaurants and discos. The discos are open until six or seven o'clock in the morning - in fact, Buenos Aires never sleeps! Now I go back to Buenos Aires as often as possible. I've been there three times, and last year I went there for New Year's. What I particularly like about Buenos Aires are the people. Argentinian people are very special. They're loud, energetic, and a lot of fun. I love them!

1.19

**a** Where are you from?
**b** I'm originally from England.
**c** Where exactly?
**d** A small town just outside Manchester.
**e** Manchester's in the north.
**f** I live in New York, but actually I'm from Los Angeles.
**g** Which part of the city are you from?
**h** Not far from the airport.
**i** They live in the south.

## Unit 3

1.20

**(W = Walt; B = Betty)**

**B:** We first met fifty years ago.
**W:** I joined the Navy and I went to Annapolis, Maryland, for my training. On the first day I went to the canteen, and this little lady was serving lunch.
**B:** Yes, I was. I liked him so I gave him extra fries.
**W:** Anyway, we started talking. Then, one night, there was a party.
**B:** I said to Walt, "I'll be your girl tonight," and that was it.
**W:** Yes, we dated for three wonderful months.
**B:** We did.
**W:** Then we both moved to different places. At first we wrote to each other. We wrote twice a week.
**B:** Yes, but then we stopped. I don't know why. But we lost touch with each other. Then we got married to other people. I had two children, and Walt had a daughter.
**W:** That's right. I was married for forty-eight years, and then my wife died.
**B:** And I got divorced after thirty years of marriage.
**W:** So we were both single again.
**B:** And one day, my grandson took me to Annapolis for the day. I visited all the old places and I thought about Walt. I wanted to find him.
**W:** She didn't even know whether I was alive.
**B:** No, I didn't. So I wrote a letter to the editor of the local newspaper.
**W:** I have a cousin in Annapolis. She doesn't usually buy the newspaper, but on that day she did. She bought the paper and she saw the letter. And she realized that Betty was looking for me.
**B:** He called me. I nearly had a heart attack. I said, "Is that my Walt?" I was so happy.
**W:** We met soon after that. We realized we were still in love and we moved in together a few months later.
**B:** We got married last summer. I didn't want to lose him again!

1.21

**1** keep – kept
mean – meant
meet – met
**2** begin – began
drink – drank
ring – rang
**3** bring – brought
buy – bought
catch – caught

1.22

**1** read – read
sleep – slept
**2** sing – sang
swim – swam
**3** fight – fought
teach – taught

1.23

**(B = Bobby; R = Rosie; D = Dave)**

It's time for our popular competition on *Get Personal*, with your host, Bobby Brown.

**B:** Good evening and welcome to this week's *Get Personal*. Let's meet our first couple, Rosie and Dave. As you know, Rosie and Dave are in separate studios - Rosie can't hear Dave, and Dave has no idea what Rosie is saying. But they can both hear me. OK, are you ready to play *Get Personal*?
**R&D:** Yes, Bobby.
**B:** OK, we'll start with you, Rosie. We want you to remember exactly what was going on when you first met Dave. OK?
**R:** OK, Bobby.
**B:** Now, Rosie, how did you first meet Dave?
**R:** Well, I was working as a nurse, and Dave was my patient. He came into the hospital for an operation.
**B:** OK, Rosie. I want you to think about the moment when you first met. What time of day was it?
**R:** Um, I was working nights that week. So early evening.
**B:** Uh-huh. And how was the weather?
**R:** I think it was raining. Yes, it was raining when I arrived at work.
**B:** What were you both wearing when you saw each other for the first time?
**R:** Now that's easy. I was wearing my nurse's uniform, a white coat, and he was wearing pajamas. Blue pajamas. Or were they green? No, blue.
**B:** Finally, who spoke first and what did he or she say?
**R:** Dave spoke first. In fact, he shouted at me. He said, "Nurse, I'm going to throw up."
**B:** Well, that's very romantic! Thank you, Rosie.

1.24

**(B = Bobby; D = Dave)**

**B:** Now, Dave, it's your turn. Where and how did you first meet?
**D:** Well, I went into the hospital for an operation, and Rosie was working there as a nurse.

**B:** What time of day was it?
**D:** Oh, I don't know. Lunchtime? No, hold on, it was later than that. Early evening.
**B:** How was the weather?
**D:** It was summer, so I guess the sun was shining.
**B:** What were you both wearing when you saw each other for the first time?
**D:** Rosie was wearing her nurse's uniform, a white coat, and she was also wearing nice perfume. I was wearing my favorite blue pajamas.
**B:** Finally, Dave, who spoke first and what did he or she say?
**D:** Rosie spoke first. She said, "How are you feeling?" And I think I said, "I feel terrible."

1.25

1 Jake was taking a shower. His cell phone rang.
2 Fiona and her friend were talking at a club. A man asked Fiona for a dance.
3 Jake and Fiona were having dinner. Jake asked Fiona to marry him.
4 Jake and Fiona were sleeping. The baby started to cry.
5 Jake and Fiona were having an argument. Somebody arrived.

1.26

How I met my husband is a funny story. Three years ago, he tweeted that he was moving and he had lots of horror DVDs he wanted to give away. At the time, we weren't following each other on Twitter, but a friend showed me his tweet.
I am a huge horror movie fan, so I agreed to come and pick up the DVDs. They were waiting on the front porch when I got to his house, but he wasn't at home.
I tweeted to say "thank you". He replied and asked me out for a coffee. He's a writer, so he said he was writing a book and he wanted to interview me for it. I met him, and he asked me all sorts of questions about my business.
At the end of the meeting he then asked me if I would like to go out for dinner with him any other day. I had to laugh! I really thought he wanted to interview me and that was it. After we were seeing each other for a few months, I asked him when he was planning to write the book ...
That's when he told me there was no book! He just wanted to make sure I wasn't crazy before asking me out. And he has his DVDs back because ... we got married last June!

1.27

Last year, Bill and Lisa were invited to a dinner party to help celebrate their fiftieth wedding anniversary. That evening, as they walked back from the party, Lisa said something very surprising.
"I'm bored, Bill. Really bored. We do the same things over and over. Couldn't we do something crazy one day?"
At first, Bill was shocked and angry. When he got back home, he went out to the garden and stared at the plants unhappily. Then he drank a big glass of water. That night, Bill couldn't sleep. Why hadn't Lisa ever mentioned that she was bored?
The next morning, Bill had a plan.
"Okay, Lisa. Let's never be bored again!"
Next, he gave her a pair of scissors.
"Go upstairs. Any clothes you are bored of? Cut them up!"
After Lisa came down with a big grin, and an even bigger plastic bag filled with cut up clothes, Bill led her to the shed.
"Okay, choose a can of paint."
Lisa chose one that was pink. A week later, their boring white house was a beautiful bright pink!
One day, Bill and Lisa went to the airport, looked quickly at the departure board, chose a destination, and bought two tickets. They spent two happy weeks there!
At the end of August this year, Bill and Lisa celebrated their fifty-first wedding anniversary ... by going to a nightclub for the first time in decades. They danced all night!

1.28

**(T = Tim; A = Anna)**
**T:** Excuse me. Do you know what time we arrive in Atlanta?
**A:** Yes, I think we get there at about 2:30.
**T:** Thanks. I see you're reading *Pride and Prejudice*. Are you enjoying it?
**A:** Yes, I am.
**T:** I didn't like the movie.
**A:** Oh, I did. I thought it was great. I really like Keira Knightley.
**T:** Oh, so do I. I think she's really good in *Pirates of the Caribbean*.
**A:** Me, too. I love that movie. Johnny Depp's fantastic.
**T:** I know. I'm going to see his new movie tomorrow night.
**A:** Really? So am I. Where are you going to see it?
**T:** At the AMC Phipps Plaza.
**A:** Me, too!
**T:** Oh, that's great. I don't know what time it starts.
**A:** No, neither do I. But my husband has the tickets, so he knows.
**T:** Oh. That's good.

1.29

a I didn't like the movie.
Neither did I. / Me, neither.
Oh, I did.
b I really like Keira Knightley.
So do I. / Me, too.
Oh, I don't.
c I think she's really good.
So do I. / Me, too.
Oh, I don't.
d I'm going to see Johnny Depp's new movie.
So am I. / Me, too.
Oh, I'm not.
e I don't know what time it starts.
Neither do I. / Me, neither.
Oh, I do.

1.30

a My name is Petra and I'm twenty-three years old. I work as a designer in a web marketing company. I'm a bit shy, and don't go out much. I like French movies. I don't like expensive restaurants.
b I'm Stevie. I'm twenty-four. I work as a sales manager for a sportswear company. I'm very loud and confident! I love watching sports. I don't like going to fancy places and wearing formal clothes.
c Hi, my name's Donny. I'm thirty-two. I own a car rental company. I guess I'm a little bit boring, I'm afraid, as I take my work very seriously. I like going to new places. I don't like loud music.

## Review A

1.31

a annoyed, Chinese, dessert, surprised
b central, cousin, Cuba
c beautiful, chocolate, finally, granddaughter, uniform
d cathedral, Egyptian, extremely, together

1.33

**(C = Carol; J = Jennifer)**
**C:** OK, so who's that in this picture, Jennifer?
**J:** Oh, that's my friend, Matt.
**C:** Friend? Really?
**J:** OK, boyfriend!
**C:** Hmm. Where did you meet him?
**J:** At college in California - about five years ago.
**C:** Oh, OK.
**J:** Yeah. I didn't actually like him at first. And I already had a boyfriend. But one day, a group of us spent the day together at the beach. We went swimming and talked and I discovered that Matt was a very interesting person and he really liked traveling.
**C:** You like traveling too, don't you?
**J:** Yes, I love it. Anyway, we talked all evening, and after that we became really good friends. But after college he went back home to Australia - he's Australian - and I stayed here.
**C:** Oh, no!
**J:** Then Matt and I started emailing and calling each other a lot because we wanted to go scuba diving in Egypt with friends.
**C:** Ah. In the Red Sea?
**J:** That's right. Anyway, I saw Matt in Egypt with all our friends. It was a lot of fun. Then, last summer, I went to Australia to visit him. I asked him to come back to the USA with me, and he did.
**C:** Really? That's wonderful.
**J:** Yes, we're good together. In fact, we're planning a trip to the Bahamas right now ... Hey, life is good!

## Unit 4

1.35

A grapes, pots, socks
B bars, keys, ties
C bridges, bunches, pieces

1.36

The last gift I bought was for my sister. It was her birthday. In fact, it was her thirtieth birthday. Thirty isn't very old, but she was pretty upset. She liked being in her twenties, and she thought thirty was really old. Anyway, I didn't know what to get her, so I went on the internet to find something. I didn't have any ideas, but I wanted something special. Eventually, I found a really good present. I thought it was unusual, and just perfect for her - it was a foot spa. My sister's a teacher and she stands up all day, so a foot spa is great for relaxing in the evening. It was expensive - about $50 - but she's my sister, and thirty is a special birthday. I bought a nice card and wrote a funny message in it - I put, "Now that you're thirty, you're too old to die young!" Ha-ha. On her birthday, I gave her the gift, but unfortunately she didn't like it - at all. She said that a foot spa is a gift for a grandmother, not for a young woman. I was really surprised - I'd love a foot spa. And then, when she read the card, she cried! What a disaster.

1.37

**(I = Interviewer; C = Conor; J = Jim)**

**I:** OK. Question one. Do you mind going to the shopping mall?
**C:** Not really. But after about an hour, I want to go home.
**J:** Actually, I can't stand going to the mall. My girlfriend knows this, so she usually chooses to go without me.
**I:** OK. Um, let's see. Question two. What kind of stores do you enjoy going into?
**C:** Bookstores. I spend a lot of time reading book reviews so I always have a list of books I'd like to buy.
**J:** I enjoy looking at electronic equipment but I can't afford to buy it. It's usually way too expensive.
**I:** OK. Question three. Are there any kinds of stores you hate going into?
**C:** I hate grocery stores. I usually forget to buy the things I went there for, so I avoid going into them. Fortunately, I can do most of my food shopping online.
**J:** I refuse to go into shoe stores. I always decide to buy shoes online. It's easier and very straightforward.
**I:** OK. Last question. Question four. Do you enjoy buying clothes for yourself?
**C:** Not really. I only go into a clothing store when I need to buy a new shirt or something. For me, shopping is a necessity, not a pleasure.
**J:** I love having new clothes, but I never manage to find time to go shopping.

1.38

Heidi is wearing a striped green linen top, a blue leather skirt, colorful plastic earrings, and white and red leather boots. All these items are on sale NOW – click here to get the look.
Ivan is wearing a black cotton shirt, a red silk scarf, a brown woolly jacket, black denim pants and black leather shoes. All these items could be yours TODAY – click here to get the look.

1.39

**a** A red woolen hat.
**b** Patterned silk ties.
**c** A pinstriped jacket.
**d** A checked shirt.

1.41

**(SC = Sales Clerk; R = Russell)**

**SC:** Can I help you?
**R:** I'm just looking, thanks. Well, actually, I'm looking for something for my girlfriend.
**SC:** What sort of thing are you looking for?
**R:** I don't really know. A sweater?
**SC:** OK, and what color would you like?
**R:** What colors do you have?
**SC:** We have any color you want, sir. Purple is very fashionable right now.
**R:** Purple's fine.
**SC:** OK. What size is she?
**R:** Ah, well, she isn't very big, but she's not particularly small.
**SC:** So she's medium.
**R:** Yes, medium.
**SC:** Well, we have this nice purple sweater here ...
**R:** Good. I'll take it.
**SC:** Are you sure you don't want to see any more ...?
**R:** No, that's great. I'll take it. Thank you. How much is it?
**SC:** That's $70, sir. How would you like to pay?
**R:** Seventy?! By credit card, please.
**SC:** Fine. If you could insert your code, please.
**R:** Here you go. Goodbye.
**SC:** Just a minute, sir. Here's your receipt.
**R:** Oh, yes, er ... Can she exchange it if it doesn't fit?
**SC:** Yes, but she needs to keep the receipt.

1.42

**(W = Woman; M = Man)**

**W:** Paul, can you go to the mall for me?
**M:** Well ... yes ... but I only have, like 20 minutes as I have to go pick Emily up.
**W:** I'm sure it won't take too long.
**M:** Okay, what do you need?
**W:** I need some shampoo - I think there's a drugstore on level 3.
**M:** Right. Shampoo.
**W:** Emily has a party tomorrow so I need some ribbon and wrapping paper. I think there's a stationery store either on level 1 or level 2.
**M:** Any color?
**W:** It's for Emily, right? It's going to be pink! I also need a bunch of flowers as a gift to Larry and Susie. There's a flower shop somewhere there ...
**M:** Okay. A bunch of flowers. Is that it?
**W:** Could you pick up some muffins and a coffee at the coffee shop? Oh, and can you see if my new phone is ready to pick up at the phone store?
**M:** You know I only have 20 minutes, right?
**W:** I'm sure you can do it. Thanks, hon!

## Unit 5

1.43

When I was in high school, we did sports every Wednesday afternoon. Two hours, from 1:30 to 3:30. Wednesdays were my worst day of the week. I hated doing sports at school. In summer we did swimming and tennis, and in winter we did lacrosse. I really, really hated lacrosse. It was always cold when we played lacrosse, but we wore shorts! Horrible, gray shorts. My legs were very thin and they were so cold that they turned blue. I was always happy when it was raining or snowing - then we stayed inside and did dancing. I loved that. At my school we had a sports field, tennis courts, and a swimming pool. I love swimming, but the swimming pool wasn't heated so it was freezing. I didn't like my gym teacher, and she didn't like me. Her name was Ms. Rockham. We called her Rocky. She looked like a boxer, and she had a very loud voice. She loved lacrosse. In fact, I think she played for the national lacrosse team. Of course, I didn't play for the school lacrosse team, but I loved dancing so much that I joined a dance club after school. My best sports moment was when my dance club won a competition for disco dancing. Rocky didn't think that dancing was a real sport, but I disagree. Dancing kept me in shape, and I didn't have to wear gray shorts.

1.44

The soccer player Ronaldo is the oldest. He was born in 1985. Amazingly, he has the same birthday as Neymar, though Neymar was born in 1992. Maria Sharapova is the next oldest - the tennis star was born in 1987. Two other stars with the same birthday, March 14, are the NBA star Stephen Curry, born in 1988, and the gymnast Simone Biles, born in 1997. And finally the golfer Rory McIlroy was born in 1989.

1.45

**(W = Woman; M = Man)**

**M:** OK, what are we looking for exactly?
**W:** We're looking for the new face of "Isotonic," the new energy drink.
**M:** Yes, I know ... but what kind of face are we looking for?
**W:** Ah, well, we need a sports star. Someone good-looking and healthy.
**M:** Good. Do we have any ideas?
**W:** Yes, we're thinking of Maria Sharapova or Rory McIlroy.
**M:** Hmm, Sharapova, tennis is more popular than golf. McIlroy ...
**M:** Hmm. I think we need someone younger. How about Simone Biles? She is not as old as Sharapova.
**W:** I don't know... How about Stephen Curry?
**M:** Who's he?
**W:** He's an NBA star - he's young, successful ...
**M:** But NBA is too American. We want this man to be the face of "Isotonic" globally. Soccer is much more popular than basketball. Who else? Neymar, Ronaldo ...?
**M:** Neymar is much younger than Ronaldo so he could be more successful in the future.
**W:** Hmm.
**M:** OK, who's your favorite sports star?
**W:** Oh, Ronaldo. I think he's the best-looking, most interesting, most talented sportsman in the world.
**M:** Well, let's use him then. Perfect. I want you to get in touch with him immediately.

1.46

a London is not as wet as Rome.
b Hawaii isn't as big as Cuba.
c The Mall of America is much smaller than the Dubai Mall.
d Heathrow Airport in London is a little bit busier than Los Angeles International Airport.
e Big Ben is a little bit taller than the Statue of Liberty.

1.47

a It's as light as a feather.
b He's as free as a bird.
c They're as good as gold.
d She's as pretty as a picture.
e It's as solid as a rock.
f It's as old as the hills.

1.48

Three quarters.
Point two five.
Point three three.
One and a half.
An eighth.
A quarter.
One point five.
Point one two five.
A third.
Point seven five.

1.49

a Two hundred and sixty-three kilometers an hour
b Forty-two point one nine five kilometers
c Seventy million, six hundred thousand dollars
d Thirty-one-nil

1.50

**(M = Man; W = Woman)**

**M:** We all know the expression "laughter is the best medicine." But a recent study shows that adults don't laugh enough. The study shows that young children laugh up to four hundred times a day, while adults only laugh seventeen times a day. According to medical research, fifteen to twenty minutes of laughter a day really does keep the doctor away.
Well, now you can join one of the laughter clubs to get your regular twenty minutes of laughter. It sounds funny, and it even looks a little funny, but this is a laughter club. Avril is the teacher here. Avril, how did the laughter clubs start?
**W:** They started in India eleven years ago. Dr. Kataria started a club in Mumbai, and now there are hundreds of laughter clubs all over the world. In India, people are very serious about the benefits of laughter.
**M:** And what are the benefits of laughter?
**W:** When you laugh, you release happy chemicals - endorphins. This can reduce the effects of stress and you feel more relaxed. Laughter boosts the immune system and relaxes the mind. Also, laughing is good for the heart and good for the lungs.
**M:** What happens in a laughter club? What exactly do you do?
**W:** We just laugh.
**M:** Do you listen to funny stories?
**W:** Oh, no. We don't need anything to make us laugh. We do exercises, and when you start laughing, you can't stop.
**M:** What kind of exercises?
**W:** Well, we start the class with a laughing exercise called Ho Ho Ha Ha Ha. After that, we do different kinds of laughing. There's "social laughter" ... "silent laughter" ... and the loud, explosive laugh ... which exercises the lungs.

1.51

**a**
**Man:** OK, are you ready?
**Woman:** Yes.
**Man:** Stand up on the board.
**Woman:** OK. Ohhhh!
**Man:** Ha-ha-ha!
**Woman:** Don't be mean.
**Man:** Oh, sorry. OK. Try again. Good! Great. Hold on. Don't let go.
**Woman:** Ohhhh! It's too difficult. I can't do it.
**Man:** Don't be silly. Of course you can do it. Be patient. Come on, try again.
**Woman:** I look stupid.
**Man:** Don't worry. Everyone looks stupid the first time. That's it. Be careful! Good. Now, don't go too fast, Selma. Selma! Come back!
**Woman:** Wheeee!

**b**
**Man:** OK, Jimmy, kick the ball to me.
**Boy:** Daddy, Daddy, look at me.
**Man:** Oh, that's very good, Jimmy. Now, this time, don't throw the ball - kick it.
**Boy:** Kick?
**Man:** Yes, with your foot. Look, like this.
**Boy:** Like this?
**Man:** No, no, don't pick it up - that's it. Now kick it. No, don't touch the ball with your hand. Use your foot. Yes, that's it. Ouch!
**Boy:** Are you OK, Daddy?
**Man:** Aagh!

**c**
**Woman:** OK, watch me. Throw the ball in the air. Watch the ball, and hit it. OK? Now you try. Throw the ball in the air and hit the - oh, OK, try again. This time, don't look at me - look at the ball. Throw the ball in the air. Watch the ball and, ... oh, no.
**Teenager:** I hate this stupid game. I want to go horseback riding. You're horrible.
**Woman:** Don't be rude, Rebecca. Pick up your racket and try again.

1.52

a 3 - a push-up
b 6 - a squat
c 2 - a pull-up
d 5 - a plank
e 4 - jog in place
f 1 - a lunge

1.53

Hi, I'm Tim, your personal trainer. And welcome to my six-minute workout. This is so easy to do, and can really get you into great shape!
Begin with 30 seconds of jogging in place as a warm-up. Afterwards, take a 10-second break.
Now, do two sets of lunges - each set should last for 20 seconds. Then take another 10-second break.
Right. Now onto push-ups. Do as many as you can in 1 minute and then take another 10-second break.
Pull-ups can be tricky, so use a chair to help you. Again, as many as you can in 1 minute and another break of the same length.
You're doing really well! Now, 30 seconds of squats and straight into the plank - try to hold for a minute.
And you're done ... and feeling good!

## Unit 6

1.54

**Mark, a CEO**
I think I wanted to be a soldier - I liked the uniform, and lots of boys want to be soldiers when they're young, don't they? Later on, I thought about being an engineer, but I didn't do any work at school so I couldn't go to college. In the end, I started working with my father, and now I'm the CEO of my own company, so I'm really happy with the way things turned out.

**Karen, a surgeon**
I've always wanted to be a surgeon, right from when I was a small child. It's my vocation. When I was at school, my best friend wanted to be a ballet dancer, but even then I knew what I wanted to do. There's never been a doctor in our family, but my father's a butcher, so I suppose it's similar!

**Frank, a teacher**
When I was five, I wanted to be a farmer or a vet because I loved animals. Later, I wanted to be a pilot, but my eyes weren't good enough. When I was at college, I wanted to be a snowboarder, but I wasn't good enough to be a professional. After college, I had no idea what I wanted to do, so I became a teacher, and I love it.

**Mia, a model**
My dream was to be an archaeologist. My family went on vacation to Mexico, and I loved the Pyramids and ruins so much that I became really interested in ancient history. But when I was sixteen, I had the chance to earn a lot of money as a model, so I stopped studying, and I've been working as a model for five years now. I want to start studying again when I'm thirty.

1.55

a said, read, fed, seen
b known, bought, flown, grown
c rung, sung, brought, hung
d drunk, taught, thought, fought

1.56

**(I = Interviewer; M = Mr. McClusky)**

**I:** And this week, in our regular report, we visit a department store with a difference ... Mr. McClusky, can you tell us what is so special about your department store?

**M:** Well, McClusky's is a large department store and you can find everything you want for the home here. Oh, and it stays open late on Thursdays and Saturdays.

**I:** Yes, that's right, but isn't there something special about the staff – you know – has anybody retired recently?

**M:** Ah, oh, I see. No. Nobody has retired recently, and we never force anybody to retire here.

**I:** How old is your oldest employee?

**M:** Well, that's Art. Art is our cleaner, and he's 87.

**I:** 87! And he cleans the store every day?

**M:** Well, not alone, no. He works with two other cleaners. They're not so old – Marshal's 70 and Ivy's 75 – no, 76. That's right, she's just had her birthday.

**I:** And they don't want to retire?

**M:** No, I think they enjoy the work, and it keeps them young. Also, we pay a decent salary, and they get four weeks of paid vacation a year.

**I:** So how many workers do you have who are over retirement age?

**M:** Well, we employ a staff of 105 and half of those are over 65. The young ones work in the office – we've got computers now, you know.

**I:** Really? Has the store changed much over the years?

**M:** No, not really. I started working here in 1948 and I've only had two secretaries in all that time. Barbara, my first secretary, resigned when she was 72.

**I:** Oh, why did she leave McClusky's so young?

**M:** Well, she was getting married to somebody who lived in another town.

**I:** Wow! That's amazing ... Do you think you will ever retire, Mr. McClusky?

**M:** Oh, yes. I'm almost 86! My son's going to take over the business next year. He's only 64.

1.57

My friend Hannah has the best job in the world – she's a personal trainer. She has about ten clients, and she writes an exercise program for each person. She doesn't work for anybody – she's self-employed. She starts work very early every day because some of her clients like to exercise before they go to work. I think she starts her first client at seven o'clock in the morning. I think it's a great job, because Hannah loves sports and so she gets money for doing what she loves. She earns a reasonably good salary. I think she charges $35 an hour, so her salary depends on the number of hours she works. She loves her job because she helps people get in shape and stay healthy. I'd love to do her job because she doesn't have to work in an office all day and she doesn't have to go to the gym in her free time either. She's her own boss so she can go on vacation when she wants, and she always looks fantastic in a swimsuit.

1.58

**John:** Good afternoon, everybody. Welcome to our *Volunteer Program*. I'm John, the program coordinator. Can you tell the group who you are, and what you do?

**Layla:** Hello. My name's Layla. I work for a big company and we produce high-quality audio equipment. I'm responsible for sales and promotion.

**Mike:** Good morning. My name's Mike. I just graduated from college. Right now, I'm unemployed. I'm looking for a job in publishing.

**Jack:** Hi. I'm Jack and I work as a bodyguard. I'm self-employed and I'm based in Detroit, but my job involves a lot of foreign travel. I have to take important clients safely from one place to another.

**Elise:** My name's Elise. I'm a photographer and I work for a music magazine. We're based in Detroit. I run the photography department and I'm in charge of taking pictures of rock stars and bands, so I travel a lot.

**John:** Thank you for being here. I'm sure everybody can help ...

1.59

**Sarah:** Hi, I'm Sarah. I work as a receptionist for Cutters Salon. I'm in charge of appointments and accounts.

**Charles:** I'm Charles. I'm a tour guide and I work for City Tours. My job involves taking tourists around Boston. Right now, I'm looking for a job in hotel management.

**Andrew:** My name's Andrew. I run a company called Luxe Autos. We produce expensive cars. We're based in Salt Lake City.

1.60

**(B = Beatrice; N = Nathan)**

**B:** Okay, I need to finish early today. Can you help me to do some of these tasks?

**N:** Really? I have to do lots of work already. Look – I have to finish writing this report.

**B:** Sorry, I can't help you with that – I don't know anything about sales.

**N:** But once I've finished, can you help print it out? The boss wants it on her desk before she leaves.

**B:** Okay, I can do that. But can you help with this filing?

**N:** Sorry, I'm useless at filing. But why don't you do the filing, and I'll help set up the conference room for the morning meeting.

**B:** Oh, great. Everyone needs a pen, notepad, and pack of Post-its.

**N:** But if I do that – can you make me a coffee?

**B:** Oh, no! My coffee is terrible! But I will get you some stationery supplies? Okay?

**N:** You have a deal – I need paperclips and folders.

## Review B

1.61

**a** doctor, flowers, leather, racket, sandals
**b** advice, afford, au pair, avoid, receive
**c** horrible, company, interested, quality, talented, valuable

1.62

**(T = Tom; P = Patsy)**

**T:** Patsy and I are very different ...

**P:** Yes, very different. In fact, we're complete opposites. Tom's water and I'm air. He's a Scorpio and I'm an Aquarius.

**T:** Mm, I don't really believe in all that ...

**P:** And Tom's much older than me. I think that also makes a difference.

**T:** I don't see what difference ...

**P:** The clothes he wears make him look older, too.

**T:** That's true. On the other hand, Patsy dresses like a teenager.

**P:** No, I don't. But I do enjoy finding fashionable clothes at good prices. I always buy him really good clothes, but he never wears them.

**T:** We've been married for twenty-two years ...

**P** Is it that long?

**T:** ... and sometimes we can't understand why we've stayed together ...

**P:** Yes. He likes watching sports on TV, whereas I like getting out there and playing them. I can't stand watching sports on TV.

**T:** She loves shopping, but I prefer sitting in my backyard with a newspaper.

**P:** So, why are we together? Simple – I love him. He's a good husband and a good father to our children. And he's one of the funniest people I've ever met.

**T:** I think I'm the luckiest person I know.

# Phonetic symbols

## Vowels

| | | |
|---|---|---|
| /ɪ/ | **fish** | /fɪʃ/ |
| /i/ | **bean** | /bin/ |
| /ʊ/ | **foot** | /fʊt/ |
| /u/ | **shoe** | /ʃu/ |
| /e/ | **egg** | /eg/ |
| /ə/ | **about** | /əˈbaʊt/ |
| /ɜr/ | **word** | /wɜrd/ |
| /ɔ/ | **talk** | /tɔk/ |
| /æ/ | **back** | /bæk/ |
| /ʌ/ | **bus** | /bʌs/ |
| /ɑ/ | **father** | /ˈfɑðər/ |

## Diphthongs

| | | |
|---|---|---|
| /eɪ/ | **face** | /feɪs/ |
| /ɔɪ/ | **boy** | /bɔɪ/ |
| /oʊ/ | **nose** | /noʊz/ |
| /aɪ/ | **eye** | /aɪ/ |
| /aʊ/ | **mouth** | /maʊθ/ |

## Consonants

| | | |
|---|---|---|
| /p/ | **pen** | /pen/ |
| /b/ | **bag** | /bæg/ |
| /t/ | **tea** | /ti/ |
| /d/ | **dog** | /dɔg/ |
| /tʃ/ | **chair** | /tʃer/ |
| /dʒ/ | **jazz** | /dʒæz/ |
| /k/ | **cake** | /keɪk/ |
| /g/ | **girl** | /gɜrl/ |
| /f/ | **staff** | /stæf/ |
| /v/ | **verb** | /vɜrb/ |
| /θ/ | **thing** | /θɪŋ/ |
| /ð/ | **these** | /ðiz/ |
| /s/ | **snake** | /sneɪk/ |
| /z/ | **zoo** | /zu/ |
| /ʃ/ | **shine** | /ʃaɪn/ |
| /ʒ/ | **measure** | /ˈmeʒər/ |
| /m/ | **map** | /mæp/ |
| /n/ | **name** | /neɪm/ |
| /ŋ/ | **ring** | /rɪŋ/ |
| /h/ | **house** | /haʊs/ |
| /l/ | **leg** | /leg/ |
| /r/ | **road** | /roʊd/ |
| /w/ | **wine** | /waɪn/ |
| /j/ | **yes** | /jes/ |

## Stress

Word stress is shown by underlining the stressed syllable:
*water, amazing, Japanese*.

## Letters of the alphabet

| /eɪ/ | /i/ | /e/ | /aɪ/ | /oʊ/ | /u/ | /ɑ/ |
|---|---|---|---|---|---|---|
| Aa | Bb | Ff | Ii | Oo | Qq | Rr |
| Hh | Cc | Ll | Yy | | Uu | |
| Jj | Dd | Mm | | | Ww | |
| Kk | Ee | Nn | | | | |
| | Gg | Ss | | | | |
| | Pp | Xx | | | | |
| | Tt | | | | | |
| | Vv | | | | | |
| | Zz | | | | | |

# Irregular verbs

| Infinitive | Simple past | Past participle |
|---|---|---|
| be | was/were | been |
| beat | beat | beaten |
| become | became | become |
| begin | began | begun |
| bend | bent | bent |
| bet | bet | bet |
| bite | bit | bitten |
| blow | blew | blown |
| break | broke | broken |
| bring | brought | brought |
| build | built | built |
| burst | burst | burst |
| buy | bought | bought |
| can | could | (been able) |
| catch | caught | caught |
| choose | chose | chosen |
| come | came | come |
| cost | cost | cost |
| cut | cut | cut |
| deal | dealt | dealt |
| dig | dug | dug |
| do | did | done |
| draw | drew | drawn |
| drink | drank | drunk |
| drive | drove | driven |
| eat | ate | eaten |
| fall | fell | fallen |
| feed | fed | fed |
| feel | felt | felt |
| fight | fought | fought |
| find | found | found |
| fly | flew | flown |
| forget | forgot | forgotten |
| forgive | forgave | forgiven |
| freeze | froze | frozen |
| get | got | gotten |
| give | gave | given |
| go | went | gone/been |
| grow | grew | grown |
| hang | hung/hanged | hung/hanged |
| have | had | had |
| hear | heard | heard |
| hide | hid | hidden |
| hit | hit | hit |
| hold | held | held |
| hurt | hurt | hurt |
| keep | kept | kept |
| know | knew | known |
| lay | laid | laid |
| lead | led | led |
| leave | left | left |
| lend | lent | lent |
| let | let | let |
| lie | lay | lain |
| lose | lost | lost |
| make | made | made |
| mean | meant | meant |

| Infinitive | Simple past | Past participle |
|---|---|---|
| meet | met | met |
| must | had to | (had to) |
| pay | paid | paid |
| put | put | put |
| read | read | read |
| ride | rode | ridden |
| ring | rang | rung |
| rise | rose | risen |
| run | ran | run |
| say | said | said |
| see | saw | seen |
| sell | sold | sold |
| send | sent | sent |
| set | set | set |
| shake | shook | shaken |
| shine | shone | shone |
| shoot | shot | shot |
| show | showed | shown |
| shrink | shrank | shrunk |
| shut | shut | shut |
| sing | sang | sung |
| sink | sank | sunk |
| sit | sat | sat |
| sleep | slept | slept |
| slide | slid | slid |
| speak | spoke | spoken |
| spend | spent | spent |
| split | split | split |
| spread | spread | spread |
| stand | stood | stood |
| steal | stole | stolen |
| stick | stuck | stuck |
| swear | swore | sworn |
| swell | swelled | swollen/swelled |
| swim | swam | swum |
| take | took | taken |
| teach | taught | taught |
| tear | tore | torn |
| tell | told | told |
| think | thought | thought |
| throw | threw | thrown |
| understand | understood | understood |
| wake | woke | woken |
| wear | wore | worn |
| win | won | won |
| write | wrote | written |

## Notes